RANDOM HOUSE ✷ NEW YORK

MY STORY

Journey of a

LANG LANG

WITH DAVID RITZ

Published in the United States by Random House, an imprint and
division of Penguin Random House LLC, New York.

RANDOM HOUSE and the HOUSE colophon are registered trademarks of
Penguin Random House LLC.

Originally published in hardcover in the United States by Spiegel & Grau,
an imprint of Random House, a division of Penguin Random House LLC,
in 2008.

Some names have been changed to protect the privacy
of the individuals involved.

For permission to reprint photographs, grateful acknowledgment is made
to the following: pages ii and iii, photo of keyboard by Greg
Kuchik/Photodisc/Getty Images; page 142, courtesy of the International
Tchaikovsky Competition; page 187, Lang Lang performing with
Maestro Eschenbach at Ravinia, courtesy of Jim Steere; page 234,
UNICEF Goodwill Ambassador Lang Lang is interviewed by the
media at UNICEF Headquarters © UNICEF/HQ04-0248/Susan
Markisz; page 239, UNICEF Goodwill Ambassador Lang Lang
accompanied by a group of children in the village of Mkuza in the
United Republic of Tanzania © UNICEF/HQ04-0551/Mariella Furrer.
All other photos courtesy of the author.

Library of Congress Cataloging-in-Publication Data
Lang Lang, 1982–
Journey of a thousand miles : my story / Lang Lang with
David Ritz.
p. cm.
ISBN 978-0-385-52457-5
1. Lang, Lang, 1982– 2. Pianists—Biography.
I. Ritz, David. II. Title.
ML417.L28A3 2008
786.2092—dc22
[B]   2008000732

randomhousebooks.com

Book design by Maria Carella

For my mother and father

"A journey of a thousand miles begins

with a single step."

—Lao-tzu, *The Way of Lao-tzu*
Chinese philosopher (604–531 B.C.)

CONTENTS

Journey of a Thousand Miles

Introduction

In my mind, I heard music as my mother held me in her arms, a sad melody that I can no longer remember. She was saying goodbye. I was nine years old, and I could not imagine life without her—she was the world to me. She was returning to Shenyang, and I would be staying with my father in Beijing. Shenyang was home, filled with people I knew and loved. Beijing was cold and lonely, an immense urban landscape of endless crowded boulevards. It was a city where I didn't know anybody.

A slim woman with curly hair and big dark eyes, my mother always smiled when she looked at me—even her eyes smiled. But now her face was wet with tears. I prayed she wouldn't leave.

"Enough," my father told her. "It is time that you go. Let the boy be. All this sentiment makes him weak."

"I know you're right, Lang Guoren," my mother said, sobbing. "But this is going to be hard on him. He's a sensitive child."

"He will do what he has to do. We all will."

I clung to my mother as she moved toward the door.

My father pulled me away.

The door opened.

My mother left.

"Go practice," my father told me. "We've wasted enough time today."

Music opened up the world to me, a boy from the outskirts of industrial China who today performs in a different country every week and who has no actual home, only the homes of my heart: China, my beloved motherland; Europe, the land of my musical heroes; and the United States, the land that transformed me and led me into adulthood.

Music, my primary language, is the world's universal language, yet each country speaks its own dialect. The West and the East may share much of the same technology, art, sports, fashion, and culture, yet their differences remain vast. Because of cultural expectations, even the same music can sound different here and there. In the West, classical music is an old-fashioned art superseded by rock, hip-hop, and other pop forms that speak to the young. Yet in China, a country closed off to the West during the Cultural Revolution of the 1960s and '70s, classical music is considered the new fashion. Every time I play a concert in China, 90 percent of the audience is younger than twenty years old. When I give a master class there, some families sleep on the sidewalk in order to get a seat, like teenagers do here for rock concerts. Kids in China are learning classical music, and loving it, in staggeringly high numbers. Fifty million kids in China study music, and of them thirty-six million study piano. Every public school has music classes, and half the songs the students learn come from the West. Sales of pianos are falling in the United States, but sharply rising in China.

China's love for classical music can often be naive. There's a joke I like to tell about a group of record producers who greeted the pianist Vladimir Ashkenazy in their boardroom to discuss a new recording of Chopin's waltzes. The producers sat silently until Ashkenazy asked if they should begin the meeting. "Shouldn't we wait for the composer?"

one of them asked. It makes me happy that Chinese piano students feel that classical music is so current and relevant. When a young person says to me, "Hey, Lang Lang, I know that you're on Deutsche Grammophon. I see that Mozart has a deal on that label too," I'm happy. I love the idea that the kid thinks that Mozart is alive and well. Somebody also asked me whether Beethoven plays better piano than Elise or whether Elise plays better than Beethoven (Beethoven wrote a piece called "Für Elise"). I answered, "What do you think?" I don't mind when a Chinese audience claps in between the movements of a concerto instead of waiting till the end. The love of the music is more important to me than traditional etiquette.

As I travel, I'm constantly asked questions about my music, about my childhood, and about bridging the gap between East and West. The easiest way for me to answer those questions is through my story.

My story is music: classical music, Chinese music, the music that I hear in my head . . .

My story is China: ancient China, modern China, the very spirit of China, my motherland . . .

And my story is also the West, my other home, which has welcomed me and shaped my life as an adult.

It all began when my parents discovered that I had a mind for music.

HALF

A CHILDHOOD

Revolution

The Cultural Revolution, which spread over a decade beginning in 1966, had an enormous impact on practically every person in China. I was born on June 14, 1982, some six years after the Revolution had ended, and I still felt its enormous reverberations. The Revolution was a large-scale, society-wide social and political upheaval in which all students and intellectuals, including musicians and artists, were sent away from the cities to labor on farms and learn from the peasants. Millions of professionals were forced to leave their homes. China was to be self-reliant and was closed to the West.

When I was around seven years old, I began asking my mother questions about our family's past. One night, while my father was at his job policing the nightclubs and entertainment district of Shenyang, and after I had completed my long practice session on the piano, my mother sat down next to me, handing me slices of fresh oranges and a glass of cool water. It didn't take much prodding to get her to start talking about her youth.

I loved listening to my mother's stories. Because she had been a singer and an actress at her school, she spoke theatrically, with bubbly enthusiasm and great dramatic pauses. As she told me the story of her life, and my father's, and how their lives intertwined, music in my head accompanied each tale—ever since I can remember, I have had a kind of soundtrack playing in my head, accompanying my life's most memorable moments. I heard études and concertos, sonatas and great symphonies. I heard the harmonies and counterpoints. I heard the action of the music. To me, music *was* action. And my parents' lives were action-packed, the stuff of drama and thrilling music.

"Music," said my mother, "was an early love in my life. Music always lifted my spirits and brought me joy."

Mom told me how, when she was four, her parents moved the family—her and her three brothers—from Dandong on the coast of North Korea to Shenyang in the north of China, where her father worked as a highly skilled technician in an iron plant and her mom became a bookkeeper. Her grandfather loved to sing songs from the Peking opera, so music filled the house.

"What about my grandmother?" I asked. "Why don't I know her?"

"She died of a lung disease when I was young."

"How young?" I asked.

"I was nine."

My heart started beating like crazy—I was suddenly terrified. "Will you die when I become nine?"

"Oh no, darling," she assured me. "I'll always be here with you."

"Were you scared?" I asked.

"Yes, I was afraid. Being the only daughter, I was so close to my mother. Losing her hurt a great deal. I was afraid of living without her."

"Then what happened?"

"The world went on," said my mother. "The world always goes on."

Her father excelled at his job in the ironworks factory. He invented a device that improved manufacturing efficiency, and he was rewarded accordingly. My mother went to school and did well; they were all bright students in her family. At school, she began acting in little plays, singing, and dancing. Then, in 1966, came the Cultural Revolution—and everything changed.

Mom's paternal grandfather was a landlord, even though my mother had never seen this "land." Though her father was a successful inventor and invaluable technician at the ironworks factory, he was now considered untrustworthy and was supervised closely. Rumors circulated that my grandfather was conspiring against the Cultural Revolution. Of course, the rumors were false, but they persisted. To protect Mom and her brothers from worry, her father never mentioned any of this. They only found out when a friend came to their house one day and cried out, "They have your father in the fools' parade!" My mother didn't even know what that meant, but of course she ran outside to see. On the street, a group of men was being forced to march from the factory, her father among them. They were all wearing dunces' hats and holding up big cards with words Mom didn't understand. She wanted to run to him, but he was surrounded by guards. That night her father didn't return home. She wept like an infant. When he finally showed up the next morning, she ran to him. "Why are they doing this to you?" she demanded. "Have you made a mistake?" "I have made no mistake," said my grandfather. "I have done nothing wrong. But these are changing times with new people in charge who persecute me even though they don't know me."

Her father was reinstated at the factory but was demoted, and he was no longer recognized or respected. My mother felt the community's contempt most keenly in school. Her classmates were being chosen to serve in the Red Guard, which was an honor for young boys and girls. Those selected wore a special red scarf, but because of her father Mom was forbidden to wear one. She was a good singer, though, so despite their scorn, they wanted her to perform for the school. During her performances, she was given the red scarf to wear, but when they were over, the scarf was taken from her. Boys from her school would chase her down the hall and curse at her. They never expected her to answer them, but she always did. She cursed them right back. She may have been wounded by their hatred, but she was not shy or weak. She had dreams and ambitions.

"What kinds of dreams, Mother?" I asked.

"Dreams of joining a professional dance or music group. Dreams of acting. When I was on that stage, it didn't matter what anyone thought of me—up there, I was invincible."

Mom had imagination and talent. She could feel the story behind the lyrics of songs and make that story come alive. She could transform herself into different characters. She could lose herself in a costume drama, or a song from another century, or a choreography arranged decades before her birth. Onstage she felt free, and she had high hopes of becoming a professional. The military recruited actresses and singers to entertain the troops of the People's Liberation Army. At that time, the military was the most important power, and to play before the generals was the biggest honor. My mother had every reason to believe that she would be chosen. Her teachers recommended her highly. Her colleagues all said she was the number one actress, dancer, and singer in her school. And yet she was rejected.

"My father's family were landlords, and landlords—even the granddaughters of landlords—could not be trusted during the Revolution," my mother told me. "My schooling ended, and so did my dreams . . ." My mother and her three brothers were sent away from their father—my mother to work on a farm, and her brothers to labor in different villages. One of her brothers was a talented Peking Opera singer, but his career was ended during the Revolution.

I loved listening to my mother talk. Inevitably, though, her stories would come to an end, and she would tell me to go practice. I was working on pieces by Chopin and Liszt that other students didn't attempt until they were thirteen or fourteen, and I was excited by the challenge. But as my fingers moved over the keys, my mind would move over the stories my mother had told me about my family. I was proud that she hadn't allowed the boys in her school to intimidate her. I was grateful for her strength, and I believed she was the artist she had hoped to become. I practiced to make up for her missed opportunities, until I conquered the music just as she had conquered her enemies. The music became a soundtrack to a movie about my mother.

At our small dinner table, she served me the food I loved best, hot dumplings and sauerkraut with pork. My father worked late, so she and I would often eat alone, and I would urge her to continue her stories.

She told me how she and my father had met in 1977, when they were both twenty-four years old. The Cultural Revolution had ended, and because of her excellent work on the farmland she was allowed to return to Shenyang. She had just begun her job as a telephone operator at the Institute of Science, and my father was working at a factory during the day. But my father's dream was to become a professional musician. He played the erhu, a two-stringed fiddle, the most popular traditional instrument in China, which in a traditional orchestra plays a similar role to the violin in a Western orchestra. Although his dream to enter the music conservatory had not been realized because the conservatories had been closed during the Cultural Revolution, he had found part-time work playing with an acrobatic circus band, and sometimes he traveled with them. But the job wasn't stable.

On their first date, my father took my mother to the movies to see a Russian film. Afterward, he told his friends that he was 100 percent satisfied with her appearance and her personality.

I asked my mother if she had been 100 percent satisfied with my father.

"I can't say I was—certainly not at first. My ideal man was a little taller, a little more dashing than your father, more talkative, and with a warmer personality. And a little more established in his line of work."

I asked if my grandfather liked him, and Mother couldn't help but laugh. She told me how her father had warned her, saying, "This man has no future, no profession. You will not be satisfied with him." My grandfather forbade my mother to date my father, but my dad was persistent. He kept asking my mother out. In spite of her father's disapproval, she agreed to meet Dad secretly on several occasions. One evening when she came home, her father spotted Dad walking her to the door. Infuriated, my grandfather slapped my mother across the face. According to Mom, this was the only time her father ever raised a hand to her.

After that, she stopped seeing my father, but it was as much his own doing as it was her father's. Once in a while, my father still called her; her job as a phone operator meant that he could reach her at any time. The country was filled with new hope for the future. The universities had just reopened, so my father decided to apply to the conservatory; he knew that higher education was his key to becoming a professional musician. While he studied for the entrance exams, he told my mother, "Zhou Xiulan, please understand if I don't call you for a while. I must dedicate myself fully to these tests." Naturally, my mother understood and wished him success.

My father placed number one on the first two exams, and yet he was still denied admission to the conservatory. My mother explained to me that the leaders of the conservatory found an inconsistency in my father's application. In those days you couldn't apply for admission if you were older than twenty-five. Dad was, in fact, twenty-five at the time, but a teacher advised him to put down twenty-four so that if he failed the exams, he could reapply the next year. My father followed the teacher's advice, but because he is an honest man, right below, in parentheses, he wrote, "Real age: 25." They immediately disqualified him—this, even though he had twice placed number one. I could only imagine how he suffered, to have his dreams dashed for such a stupid infraction that had nothing to do with his talent.

After that, my mother's father forbade her to see my father at all. According to my grandfather, the incident proved that Lang Guoren was not worthy of his daughter's company. Mom was told to return all the small gifts my dad had given her, and she had no choice but to obey.

"But you married him anyway," I reminded her.

"As I said, your father is a tenacious man. He would not let me go. Now that he was no longer preoccupied with his studies, he would not stop calling me at my job. On some days he must have called fifty times. He called so often I could hardly do my work. He would insist that I accompany him to a concert or a play. When I told him that my father had forbidden me, he said, 'You don't have to tell your father.' "

So a new, even more secret phase of their relationship began. It wasn't at all romantic; at first my parents were simply friends. My mother began enjoying my father's company more and more. But although she realized that they had many artistic interests in common and she saw that he was intelligent, she let him know that she did not see her future with him.

" 'Don't underestimate me, Zhou Xiulan,' Lang Guoren told me. 'I will have a good future. I'll prove it to you. I will become a professional musician.'

"Because my own artistic dream had been denied, I didn't believe him. I didn't think it was possible for him to find a stable job as an artist.

" 'I will find a job,' he said, 'and I will win your love.' "

Of course, as with anything my father put his mind to, he succeeded on both counts. The Air Force had a program for musicians to play in its band, but to enter it, you had to pass exams. The Air Force orchestra's pay was decent and the work steady. If he got in, my father would no longer have to work his two jobs, one at the factory and one in the acrobatic circus. So he found a teacher at the Shenyang Conservatory of Music to tutor him. For months he practiced his erhu day and night, outside so that he wouldn't disturb anyone, beginning at 4:00 a.m. before he went to work and until midnight after work. His discipline never faltered, and, true to his word, when the exam day came, he excelled. He was finally granted admission to the Air Force as a soloist and concertmaster of the orchestra.

Mom's father was impressed. "Perhaps I have misjudged the man, Zhou Xiulan," he said. "He is ambitious and persistent. I will no longer interfere in your friendship with him."

Their friendship blossomed into love. I didn't see my dad as a romantic man, but when my mother told the story, I understood that he had passion. My parents were married on April 22, 1980, and I was born a little more than two years later.

At first they lived with my paternal grandparents. But when Dad's younger brother married, he needed a place to live with his new bride. My father, being generous, offered his place in their parents' home. In those days, you couldn't just buy an apartment, because apartments were allocated by the state. But as an Air Force musician, my father qualified for a room in the barracks. He and my mother, who was pregnant with me at the time, could move there, and that would solve the problem. But new complications emerged: Chairman Deng Xiaoping was reforming China, and one of his goals was to reduce the size of the military; Dad learned that the Shenyang Air Force orchestra would be dismantled in a couple of years, and when that happened, he would not be entitled to a room.

So my father made a plan that defied all the regulations. He had no other choice. Mom was less than a month away from giving birth. She was big and uncomfortable, and the thought of being homeless was too much to bear, so she went along with Dad's plan. He got a truck and moved everything—the bed, dresser, clothes—without permission, into a vacant apartment in the barracks. Naturally, the leaders were furious. In the military, you cannot break rules. Some of his superiors wanted to evict them right then and there, but others were more sympathetic: How could my father move when his wife was about to give birth? Quite unexpectedly, my parents were allowed to stay, and I was born in the Air Force barracks.

My given name Lǎng means "brightness and sunshine," and my family name Láng means "educated gentleman." Though I'm grateful to my parents for having given me such a wonderful name, I now have to live up to their expectations. My birth, like so many things in my life, was a challenge. My umbilical cord was wrapped around my neck two and a half times, almost choking me to death. My face had turned a terrible shade of green, and I made no sound. But when the doctor removed the cord and slapped my behind, I cried a piercingly loud cry.

I didn't die, my mother explained to me, because I had work to do—the work of bringing music to the world. As a child of two musicians who had had their ambitions and hopes shattered, I was born of great expectations—ones that both guided me and led me to great success.

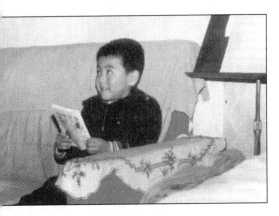

I LOVED COMIC BOOKS.

Tom and Jerry

People often ask me about my influences. They want to know the cultural forces that inspired my love of music. They expect me to say Beethoven or Brahms, Tchaikovsky or Bach. Naturally, they're shocked when I say Tom and Jerry, the beloved cartoon characters created in Hollywood.

How could an animated cat chasing an animated mouse possibly inspire me? Let me explain.

It began one morning when I was not yet two years old. It was summertime, and I was fast asleep when I awoke to a loud knock at the door. A man outside was shouting, "Delivery!"

My mother opened the door, and I stood behind her. Two men were in the hallway on either side of an enormous carton.

"What is it?" I asked my mother.

"You'll see," she said, smiling proudly.

It seemed to take forever as the deliverymen tore away the packing, ripping off endless sheets of heavy cardboard. Finally, underneath all that packing, the most beautiful object I had ever seen was revealed.

An upright piano.

I ran over and touched it. I pressed the keys. The dark wood was smooth and without a scratch. The ivories were smooth. The inscription above the keys said, "Xing Hai."

"It is yours," said my mother. "All yours."

I hugged her, and then, for the remainder of the day and well into the evening after my father returned from work, I played my piano.

Very soon after getting the piano, I saw two cartoons on our small black-and-white television set. In the first, "The Music Kingdom," musical instruments appeared on the screen and played by themselves. First came the trumpet, announcing, "I am Trumpet. I am a general because I play the overture." Then the timpani arrived and argued that they were the most powerful instrument because they made the storms and thunder, while the harp insisted that she made the most beautiful heavenly sound and the violin said that as leader of the orchestra, she was queen of the instruments. Suddenly all the instruments disappeared, and a grand piano stood alone, playing by itself. "The king has arrived," the cartoon announced. The cartoon made me proud to play the most important of instruments. But even more than "The Music Kingdom," an episode of the cartoon *Tom and Jerry* called "The Cat Concerto" made a lasting impression on me, and each time it aired, I was riveted.

Tom is a cat but also a concert pianist. He comes out in a tuxedo and bows to the audience. Then he starts to play. His playing is magnificent. A cat in a tux is playing the piano! I found it hilarious. First the music is slow. Then, inside the piano, we see that Jerry, the little mouse, is taking a nap on the strings and the felts. He wakes up and waves to Tom. He teases Tom, while Tom, determined to keep playing, ignores him. But Jerry gets under the keys and under Tom's skin. The music speeds up and so does the action. Tom and Jerry drive each other crazy: Tom gets his finger caught in a mousetrap set by Jerry; Jerry gets thrown under the piano bench by Tom. Jerry gets out and starts hitting the keys to a jazz beat in the middle of this classical piece. Cat and mouse fight furiously while the music continues. The music and the fighting are perfectly in sync. In the end, Jerry triumphs. The cat is worn out while the tiny mouse, now wearing a tux, takes a bow as the audience applauds.

I later learned that the piece the duo was playing was the Hungarian Rhapsody no. 2 by Franz Liszt. But as a baby of only twenty-one or twenty-two months, I didn't even understand what a composer was. I simply loved animated creatures, how they played with and against each other. Cat was chasing mouse. Mouse was teasing cat. Little feet were scurrying up and down the keys. I was especially impressed by Tom's fingers. He could extend them in order to reach the keys at either end of the piano. To play a key was to ignite action. To play many keys was to keep the story flowing. The faster you played, the faster the creatures chased each other, the crazier their adventures, the sillier their spills, the funnier their pranks.

Playing the piano meant pranks. It meant fun.

It was silly, it was crazy, it was slow, it was speedy, it was a merry-go-round of music.

I wanted to play the piano faster and faster, to see how fast my fingers could fly over the keys. I wanted to see how fast I could chase Tom and how quickly I could catch Jerry. I wanted to jump and fall, and then get up and do it all over again. Even if my hands grew tired and my fingers began to ache, it didn't matter, because I was making up stories by making music.

My father accompanied me on the erhu practically every day. He appreciated my playfulness and could be playful himself. He could make the erhu sing and laugh. Together, we told our own speechless stories. That's when my father and I were able to express love. It was a deep and powerful connection, but also dangerous, a love that commingled with ruthless and overwhelming ambition, forceful enough to turn a child's play into an obsession.

MY MOTHER AND ME IN OUR
ROOM IN THE BARRACKS

The Barracks

For several reasons, the fact that I was born in the Air Force dormitory has helped me become who I am today. First, I lived in an atmosphere of protection and safety. We didn't lock our doors or worry about crime, because entrance to the base was fiercely guarded; in fact, I grew up in one of the most guarded places in all of China. In that impermeable bubble, I was free to concentrate on my music without worry or distraction. Second, the campus was rich with a sense of adventure.

The military base was a thrilling playground, a won-derland of imagination to a child already inclined to lose himself in dreams of faraway places. In 1984, China was engaged in a war with Vietnam, and enormous, terrifyingly loud fighter planes would fly above us, and land and take off at the base, when I played with my friends. The sight of all those air-planes made me believe that one day I would see the world. But the best part of all was that in our section

AT THE MILITARY AIRPORT
NEXT TO THE AIR FORCE
BASE

of the barracks, the artists' quarter, music was everywhere. Every Saturday night Mom and Dad would invite our musician friends and their kids to our room for a party.

Of course, each kid was an only child. In 1979, alarmed by population growth, the Chinese government initiated a one-child policy, and so an entire generation was born blessed and cursed by completely undivided parental attention and no sibling companionship. And worse, our parents had been robbed by the Cultural Revolution—their ambitions had been stymied, and, in turn, they grafted their hopes onto us. What they couldn't achieve of their dreams, we would achieve. Where they had failed, we would succeed. Every last ounce of their energy was devoted to us; we carried the burdens and the blessings of their hopes and dreams. Chinese parents' favorite symbols of fortune for their children are the dragon and the phoenix. All parents hoped their sons would be dragons, their daughters phoenixes. As only children, we were even called "Little Prince" or "Little Princess" by our grandparents. And in the case of an obviously talented child, the pressure was even greater, the expectations higher.

Our parties in the artists' barracks were very happy affairs, but also very intense and competitive. Almost all the children played Western instruments, while their parents all improvised along with us on Chinese instruments: the erhu; the pipa, which resembles a lute; the guzheng, a Chinese harp; the suona, a kind of Chinese trumpet; and the bamboo flute. A little girl played the violin, one little boy played the erhu, but most of the children played piano. I played the piano because my dad said it was the most beloved instrument. He and my mom had been thinking that way since they had discovered my talent; even before I was one, they heard me singing melodies from the radio, and they taught me to read musical notes before I learned to read letters.

I relished playing. Even more than playing, I loved performing—showing my friends and my parents' friends the Mozart sonatina I had memorized; I loved the feeling of sharing music with others. Many of the other children were older and already proficient in their musician-ship, and I was keenly aware that I wanted to play better than they did. But my competitive nature never got in the way of the camaraderie, warmth, and generosity of our gatherings.

Still, some of the kids whispered, "Lang Lang is a show-off." I was so desperate to play one piece, and then another, and then still another; I'd play every song I knew from Bach's fugue to a piece by Liszt called the "Little Hungarian Rhapsody." Of course every child wants to dem-onstrate how well he can run or swim or play the piano. But my desire to play went beyond merely showing off: I wanted to express myself through the music.

My mother had filled our small barracks room with fresh flowers and blooming plants that smelled of mint and spice. The air was fresh and fragrant, and we would sit together playing and singing songs, which were always about maternal rivers—rivers that give sustenance and life to the people—and noble shepherds who love nature and guard the animals. Those impromptu concerts remain among the happiest memories of my childhood.

The fellowship in the barracks was strong. We ate in a common kitchen and shared common bathrooms. We were a makeshift family of artists, even us little ones, eating, singing, laughing, and playing our hearts out.

Teacher's Story

When I was four, I overheard my father speaking to Mr. Bai, the conductor of the Air Force orchestra.

"My son needs a teacher. A good teacher."

"My daughter's violin teacher has a friend who heads the piano department at the Shenyang Conservatory of Music," Mr. Bai offered. "She is the best teacher in the city."

"Will she teach my son?"

"She must first hear him play."

Later that day my father threatened me: "Now you must practice twice as hard. When you play for this teacher, you must make no mistakes. Not one. Start practicing now."

Both my parents had taught me the rudiments of reading music, but it was my father who had become my piano teacher. He had been studying piano for the past two years on a pedal organ in order to be able to instruct me. Now, though, he realized that his teaching skills were limited, and he wanted me to have the best instructor available.

I could see that his plans for me had taken on a fresh urgency, and for the first time I worried that I would disappoint him. He told me that my instructor's name was Professor Zhu Ya-Fen and that with her help I would become a good pianist, and "the only way to achieve that," he said, "is through practice. With practice you will be famous all over the world."

My first meeting with Professor Zhu was a momentous event, but the day did not begin well. My father was nervous and, of course, that made me nervous. He was afraid that my performance before my first teacher would not meet her standards and she would reject me. And if she rejected me, my career would be over before it began. According to my father, everything depended on my having the best teachers. And according to everyone, Professor Zhu was the best.

"No mistakes," he kept saying. "When you play in front of this woman, you can make no mistakes."

As I got dressed that morning, I envisioned a tall witch who would stand over me and rap my knuckles with a ruler if I played a wrong note. I was frightened. This was, after all, my first audition.

"Hurry!" my father yelled. "We must leave right now!"

My dad put me in the sidecar of his motorcycle, and we rode through the city. It was wintertime, and Shenyang was bleak, even foreboding that morning. The temperature was freezing, and while the concrete city flew by, the wind whipped me in the face. I looked out on a landscape of ironworks, with a few leafless trees. The factories were coughing up smoke. The sky was gray. Snow was falling. Even when the weather turned warm in Shenyang, the sun stayed hidden behind a layer of thick yellow smog. An industrial city of seven million people, the biggest city, in fact, in northeast China, the proud capital of the Liaoning region, Shenyang looked unhappy that morning of my first audition, frozen and stark. I was frozen too, and terrified.

But the moment I saw Professor Zhu Ya-Fen, my fear vanished. She was a small, delicate woman who looked nothing like a witch. She greeted me with a smile and helped me take off my coat and mittens. She was patient and spoke softly.

Children sense when adults like them, and I sensed immediately that Professor Zhu understood me. She complimented me on my military uniform, which was the pride of my wardrobe. She asked me gently whether the toy pistols in my belt would interfere with my playing. I took the guns out and gave them to my father to hold. She wanted to know whether I needed to use the bathroom before we got started. She asked if I was thirsty. She told me to relax.

"Relax" was a new word for me when it came to musical instruction. When I watched cartoons, I could relax. When I played the piano for fun, I could relax. But when my father was watching and evaluating my performance, relaxation was out of the question. I was afraid of not pleasing him. And today, quite naturally, I wanted to please Professor Zhu. The very utterance of the word "relax" came to me as a revelation. Relax in the face of being critiqued? Relax with the threat of rejection hanging over my head?

"Yes, child, just relax," Professor Zhu repeated. "Think of what makes you happiest, and then play."

I thought of my favorite cartoon character, Monkey King, who could overcome any obstacle, who conquered all fears and always saved the day. I relaxed. I played well.

"You are gifted," said the professor when I was finished. She touched my cheek, a gesture that reminded me of my mom. "I will give you a new exercise book and a composition to learn for next week."

"Shouldn't he learn two or three new compositions?" asked my father.

"One will be sufficient," Professor Zhu answered calmly. "There is no rush."

"What about competition?" asked my dad. "When will he be ready to enter a competition?"

"He will be ready when he is ready," said my new teacher. "And, believe me, that time will come soon enough."

Years later, after I had enjoyed some success, I asked Professor Zhu about her first impression of me.

"I had been told you were talented," she said, "but I didn't quite know what to expect." She described to me my beautiful manners, the way I bowed politely when we were introduced. She told me that she had introduced me to her mother-in-law, who shared the apartment with her and her husband. "From then on," she said, "whenever you came for your lessons, you would first proceed to my mother-in-law's room, knock on the door, and, when she opened it, greet her with a deep bow."

Professor Zhu told me that I had asked her, in a sweet, high-pitched voice, if she would like to hear me play.

"Of course I would, my child," she responded.

I marched directly to the piano, placed two pillows on the bench so that I could reach the keys, and began to play an extremely difficult exercise by Hanon. Professor Zhu told me that I played with neither hesitancy nor fear, that my relationship to the piano was like other children's relationships to toys. "You genuinely loved to play," she said. "It was a game to you, a game at which you were exceedingly skilled."

"Will you accept him as a student?" my father was quick to ask.

Professor Zhu answered just as quickly. "I told your father that I would, that you had talent. I remember that when I said that, your father did not smile. In those days, I can't remember your father ever smiling. He had questions he wanted answered—and he wanted the answers immediately."

"How talented do you think Lang Lang is?"

"Quite talented," Professor Zhu stated.

"He must be the number one piano player in all of China. And then all the world. Is that possible?" he asked her.

Professor Zhu recognized that my father, like so many parents whose lives were affected by the Cultural Revolution, was placing his hopes on me. She admired his straightforward attitude: he said what he meant and meant what he said. Professor Zhu's life had also been interrupted by the Cultural Revolution. She, her husband, and their children had been sent from their home to work as rice farmers. For many years they toiled in the fields, and my teacher was unable to play the piano. To even speak of one's love of Bach was a dangerous act at that time. Professor Zhu was raised in Shanghai by English-speaking nuns and had been taught by the most respected teacher in all of China, Madame Cui Cheng Li. Madame Cui Cheng Li had been a legendary pianist who could transpose and play Bach's *Well-Tempered Clavier* in every key. A beloved mentor and musical prodigy, she did not survive the Revolution—she tragically took her own life, as some musicians did at that time. Yet in spite of the hardships her family faced, Professor Zhu told me that their years in the rice fields were not all bad. "The farmers loved us and we loved them. They treated us kindly and taught us patiently. Patience, I learned, is the key to learning and the key to teaching. I saw how badly your father wanted you to succeed. 'Do not be easy on the boy,' he kept telling me. 'Push him. Challenge him. There's nothing he can't do. There's nothing he won't do on the piano.' "

Professor Zhu told my father that I had an astute ear, large hands with long fingers, an instinctive sense of rhythm, and a gift for sight-reading. But as important as those factors were, she believed that my most outstanding quality was my spirit. She felt that I understood the power of the music I played, could tap into the tremendous emotions within the music. "If we deal with him harshly," she told my father, "and push him without restraint, we risk endangering that spirit, even destroying it. To do so would be a crime." She told my father that while she understood his ambition for me, and even applauded it, she would always protect my spirit above all else.

My father did not understand Professor Zhu's philosophy. He always worried that she was being too easy on me. He believed I could handle anything, no matter how advanced, that I just needed to practice harder if necessary. I would practice all night if I had to.

"Children require recreation," my teacher told my father. "They require rest and play. Like plants, they require sunlight and nourishment. You can't rush their growth." But my father insisted that she keep pushing me; he insisted that she give me harder pieces to play and that I memorize them more quickly than the average child. He believed I was different from other children. "If you take it easy on him, you will hurt him," he told her. "You will compromise his progress and his future." Still, my father respected Professor Zhu, even though she did not change her approach with me; yet, as the years went on, he continued to challenge her.

Professor Zhu's patience and nurturing surely changed my life. But my father's approach, which was a reflection of the culture of our country at the time, ultimately prevailed. That approach had to do with winning, winning, winning.

Monkey King

At the age of four, my world was confined to our small room in the Air Force barracks and focused on music, cartoons, and comic books. If my horizons were expanded at all, it was because of Monkey King. He was my hero—then and now. Monkey King was a monkey, an adorable cartoon character, but he was much more than that. When I was older, I learned that he was a character from a Chinese epic novel from the sixteenth century called *Journey to the West*, which was based in turn on a story from the seventh century, during the Tang dynasty. But even as a little kid I could sense his significance. Monkey King was on a hero's mission to bring the truth to all people. He had a good heart and helped people in trouble. He was immortal. He was born of rock. He rebelled in heaven. He was buried under a mountain for five hundred years and only managed to escape when he agreed to protect a monk on the monk's pilgrimage to bring the holy Buddhist texts through India to China. He was more powerful than any other creature in the world; no one could catch him—he had incredible strength and speed. But though he took his assignment seriously, he also played pranks and had fun. He could change forms. He could turn into a fish, a flea, a turnip, or a tree. But whenever he transformed, he always kept his tail—that made me laugh.

Like music, Monkey King took on many different shapes that suggested countless different stories. But in every story Monkey King knew who was good and who was bad. He protected children, monks, and good people. One of his companions was an adorable pig, a former general of the Sky Palace who was turned into a pig because of his womanizing; he could not control his temper or his appetite. If you weren't looking, he would eat all your food. But you forgave the pig, just as you forgave Monkey King, because he had a good heart and they were both on a great journey to bring joy to people.

Early on I knew about Superman. He was popular in China: he could fly, he was all-powerful, he apprehended the bad guys. But Monkey King was better because he did not fall for women—he had no need of a love life. His loves were his adventures. He had monkey problems, but he could still crush anyone who threatened him. Even the Chinese gods feared Monkey King. Freed from his captivity under the mountain, Monkey King always redeemed himself from any mischief he had done. For all his crazy adventures, his message was about redemption and peace. Monkey King made me feel brave. As a little boy, I did not draw well, except for Monkey King. I was an expert illustrator of Monkey King and never tired of depicting him.

My friend Mark Ma, whose Chinese name was Zhi Jia (he later moved with his parents to America and changed his name) and who also lived in the Air Force barracks, loved Monkey King as much as I did. He and I loved playing with new Atari games from Japan that his father would buy him, or looking at *Dragon Ball Z*, Japanese comic books. Mark had the best collection of comic books and trading cards of any kid I knew. He also had the most Transformers, those toys that change from ordinary machines to robots just by twisting and turning their parts. For example, a truck could turn into a fighter jet. Like

Monkey King, Transformers captured my imagination because they could tell stories. There were the good Transformers and the bad Transformers. The car men were good; they protected the world. The sky men were bad; they wanted to destroy it. Deadly battles were fought. Robots became motor vehicles, and motor vehicles became robots. This business of transforming—of magically becoming something and someone different from who you are—fascinated me.

When I played the piano, I became something different, something more extraordinary than just a boy. Like Monkey King and the Transformers and *Tom and Jerry*, the piano took me away from one world and transported me into another, where I was happier. I became a character like Monkey King, a force that could not and would not be defeated. I imagined myself flying across the globe in one of the planes that were housed at the Air Force base, armed with guns to fight off my enemies. I liked living at the military base—the equipment excited me, the planes most of all. Flying was mysterious, and airplanes were the most thrilling form of transportation because they were the fastest. At the start of a new composition at the piano, I imagined myself taking off, lifting off, leaving the ground.

Despite how little time I had for them, I never truly set Tom and Jerry and Monkey King and Transformers aside. I worked them into the rhythms and dramatic movements of the pieces I played. Beethoven didn't have a Transformer in mind when he composed, but who cared? Who even understood that Beethoven was a Western European who had lived and died long ago? As far as I was concerned, Beethoven had written the score for a movie starring robots and monsters, anti-aircraft guns, and nuclear submarines. Monkey King even helped me play Mozart. Mozart wrote music almost as mini-dramas; every few bars a new character enters his pieces, each of a different age, nationality, or temperament. Since Monkey King was always transforming, every few bars I came to see him inhabiting Mozart's compositions.

Thus, with the help of Monkey King and an ever-expanding cast of characters and military hardware, I made progress at the piano by leaps and bounds. I didn't like learning scales and tackling exercise books, but I did so because I realized that to play the pieces that I loved—to be able to run over the keys like Tom chasing Jerry—I needed to practice. In that way, even as a small child, I was practical. Still, I made a game out of practicing. And my mother helped me by cutting out gold-colored stars; when I memorized a piece or played something particularly well, she'd give me a star. When I received five stars, she bought me a new toy. My instincts told me that playing was playing, whether playing with Transformers or playing pieces by composers whose names I could not pronounce.

FIRST PIANO COMPETITION,
AGE FIVE

Field of Rivals

"Number One" was a phrase my father—and, for that matter, my mother—repeated time and time again. It was a phrase spoken by my parents' friends and by their friends' children. Whenever adults discussed the great Chinese painters and sculptors from the ancient dynasties, there was always a single artist named as Number One. There was the Number One leader of a manufacturing plant, the Number One worker, the Number One scientist, the Number One car mechanic. In the culture of my childhood, being best was everything. It was the goal that drove us, the motivation that gave life meaning. And if, by chance or fate or the blessings of the generous universe, you were a child in whom talent was evident, Number One became your mantra. It became mine. I never begged my parents to take off the pressure. I accepted it; I even enjoyed it. It was a game, this contest among aspiring pianists, and although I may have been shy, I was bold, even at age five, when faced with a field of rivals.

The determination to win was in my blood. It *is* in my blood. It shaped my dreams at night and drove my discipline during the day.

"It is not wishful thinking," my father would say. "It is not an idle hope or a silly prayer. Being Number One is a realistic goal to be achieved through dedication. You may face a competitor who has more talent than you. You can't control that, though I believe you have all the talent and creativity you need. But you *can* control how hard you work. You can make sure that you work harder than anyone."

It was much later in my life that I learned where my father's motivation originated.

Dad was born on March 5, 1953. In those days, patriotism implied unconditional dedication to work and economic progress; my father was called Lang Guoren because the name—"guo" means "the nation," and "ren" means "duty"—suggested duty to his country. Unconditional dedication to my career became my father's solemn duty.

My great-grandfather was a famous educator and the founder of a school in northeast China. His son, my grandfather, became an accountant and a music teacher; he played many instruments but was especially talented at the harmonica. My grandmother was also an educated woman who became the director of a trade union. As a young couple with five children, they faced the economic difficulties plaguing our country. Food was scarce. Natural disasters, including a devastating flood, threatened their very existence. But they managed to hold on.

My grandfather taught my father music, just as my father taught me. But just as my father was ultimately unable to forge a career as a musician, neither was his father. He took work in a factory, and though he excelled in that work, he suffered during the Cultural Revolution.

One day my grandfather didn't come home from work. The next morning, concerned and afraid, Dad and his brother went to the plant where their father had enjoyed a spotless record and were surprised to find proclamations denouncing him on the factory walls. They had taken him away. For many weeks Dad lived in fear that his father would never return.

After a month or so, my grandfather reappeared. Dad and his family were grateful to have him back, and grateful that they were not relocated to a farm, but they were carefully watched because one of my grandfather's brothers, whose family later moved to the United States, was a Nationalist and had fled to Taipei. Having even one family member leave the mainland for political purposes put the entire family under lots of pressure. When the restrictions were lifted, my grandfather was too old to take advantage of a new world of opportunities, but Dad wasn't. Dad was still young with a big musical talent. He felt he must emerge victorious from every single battle. No combat could be lost. No result could be anything less than Number One.

In that way, my father's heart and my own heart beat as one. And when I was five, we were determined that I would win my first contest.

"Your heart was set on winning," Professor Zhu told me many years later. "I was afraid it was too early for you to start competing. I saw how you were growing tense, and I didn't like that. You were only five! But your father was insistent and, in your own way, so were you. You would have been crushed had I not prepared you to win the contest."

It was a big contest, too. Over five hundred children, most of them older than I was, had already submitted their applications by the time I applied. Professor Zhu had given me a variation by Kabalevsky, the Russian composer, a piece she thought would impress the judges, and I was excited when I saw it. It was advanced, but I realized that I could master it. But when I played it for my teacher the first time, I was overexcited and lost my balance.

"Lang Lang," she told me, "if you play the piece this way for the judges, you won't advance beyond the first round."

When I heard those words, tears began to stream down my cheeks. In my mind, I had already lost.

"But don't be discouraged," she added. "I can show you what you're doing wrong and how to avoid those mistakes."

With that, my face lit up and the tears stopped.

"Show me," I said. "Please show me right now, Professor."

It was a matter of tempo, of relaxation, and of approaching the piece more musically. It meant hard work and tedious practice, but I was elated that there was an answer to my problem. I practiced twice as hard. I conquered the Kabalevsky variation, a composition that would have been challenging for someone three times my age. At five years old, I entered my first official competition, the Shenyang Piano Competition, a citywide contest for all piano students under the age of ten, and won first prize. Afterward, I gave my first recital. In 1987, China still didn't know how to perform Western pieces; I was dressed in Peking opera makeup, with a red face and heavy eye makeup. I looked like a little cat. I loved being onstage with the warm lights on me and the passionate applause from the audience. The stage felt like a sweet home to me. Right at that moment, I decided to be a concert pianist.

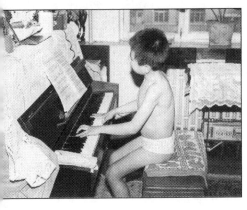

Number One

My imagination was vivid because I spent so much of my early childhood alone. Now that I had won my first competition and was determined to be a pianist, I no longer wanted to go to school. I didn't like the kindergarten classes or teachers. And when I wanted to leave early to go home and practice, they wouldn't let me. They didn't understand me. I was a shy boy who was uncomfortable outside my home, but I couldn't remain home alone. Both Dad and Mom worked. After her long maternity leave—in those days you were given a hundred days with pay—my mother had returned to her job as a telephone operator. Very fortunately, my seventy-eight-year-old great-grandmother traveled from another city to come to take care of me for three years. After she left, I was convinced I could stay alone, so I came up with an idea.

"Get a tape recorder," I told my father, "and turn it on when you and Mom leave in the morning. I'll practice all day. When you get home, you can check the recorder and see that I've kept my promise."

Dad liked the idea because it kept me at the piano. I liked the idea because it kept me from school. At the piano, even tackling impossible-to-play pieces by Czerny, seemingly designed to drive a pianist crazy, I never felt as awkward as I did in the classroom. Mom's job and its flexible hours allowed her to come home from time to time to check on me. When she did, I was always at the piano, practically anchored to it. Despite being alone during the day, I felt no fear. Sitting on that stool, conquering difficult pieces, I felt in control. And completely safe. After all, I was on a guarded military base. What could happen to me?

But because I was alone so much of the time, my natural shyness intensified. When grade school began and I could no longer stay home, the idea of returning to class terrified me. I was so uncomfortable with other kids that I pretty much stayed to myself, and that's why I was happy to run home at lunchtime to practice. My father had set up a daily routine for me that didn't allow much time for recreation:

5:45 a.m.: Wake up and practice piano for an hour.

School at 7:00 a.m.

Home at noon for lunch: Fifteen minutes for eating; forty-five minutes for practicing.

After school, two hours of practice before dinner.

Dinner: Twenty minutes, during which I watched cartoons.

Two hours of practice after dinner.

Homework.

My father was all business when it came to me and the piano. The only time he relaxed was when he played his erhu. Then something in him changed. He looked different. He lost himself in the haunting sadness of his music, as if he were looking for something that could never be found. My father made the erhu cry.

When I heard Dad play, I closed my eyes. If I saw Tom and Jerry, I saw them crying as well. Maybe they were lost and couldn't find their way home. Maybe their mothers had died. When I played, I always told happy stories, but my father told a sad one. I wanted to know more about his story, but the mystery of the sadness stayed inside the notes. Unlike my mother, my father talked very little about himself.

I consoled myself with stories of Monkey King and the Transformers, of Tom and Jerry and Donald and Daisy Duck, and of the colorful Japanese comic books filled with explosions and chases and fabulous monsters. And there were the stories in the music, the ones I made up in my mind as I practiced and played by myself or in front of my father or my teacher. But there were also the stories of the composers. I had no idea that they had lived long ago in countries whose languages were not my own. When my father and my teacher began explaining to me that these men were dead, I was totally confused.

The first question I asked my dad was: "Of all the composers, who is Number One?"

"Mozart," he was quick to say. "Mozart is Number One because he wrote the most and he wrote the best. He could compose when he was three. He was a super-genius who created masterpieces in every form. He wrote concertos and symphonies and operas. He wrote the most beautiful melodies and the most moving rhythms. He wrote with the biggest imagination and the most pleasing harmonies. He wrote for princes and kings. He began playing when he was barely more than a baby, and he had a father who watched over him and helped bring his music to the world. His father was nearly as famous as Mozart. Were it not for Mozart's father, Mozart would not have become famous. Together, they achieved immortality." My father clearly identified with Mozart's father.

My father explained to me something about the background of the courts of Austria during Mozart's day. I'm not sure how much I really understood, but when I played Mozart, I had a picture of who he was and how he behaved. I envisioned him as a character in a cartoon who loved to run and skip. He chased his friends around the playground and they chased him. Unlike cold and polluted Shenyang, the Vienna of my mind was golden, and Mozart was a golden boy who danced from one birthday party to another.

Bach was different. Professor Zhu loved Bach most and played him magnificently. She taught me his pieces from the very beginning of our time together, and the strength of his music shook me to my core. I was lucky to encounter Bach early because Bach is the foundation for music; learn Bach and you learn music. His many complex melodic lines and voices help you understand the structure of music. When I pictured Bach, he was always talking to God in heaven, and though he was somber, their conversations yielded the most beautiful and most intellectual music imaginable.

I imagined Chopin as a handsome man, a movie idol, who always sought a love he could never find. I saw him crying as he sat at his piano and wrote those heartbreaking melodies.

Beethoven was another hero of mine. He was serious, as serious as my father. Neither my father nor Beethoven ever smiled; they didn't have the time or patience to party or joke or watch cartoons. There was music to write and music to learn, and music was a matter of life and death. For Beethoven, music was grand. My father and Beethoven related more to music than they did to people.

I fell in love with Tchaikovsky when my parents took me to a performance of *Swan Lake* by a Russian ballet company, but that love deepened immeasurably when I heard his Piano Concerto no. 1. Of course I was far too young to identify it as such, but the rich emotions of his Russian soul spoke to my impressionable mind. I saw him living alone in a big house; I pictured him weeping and writing, writing and weeping. The beautiful melancholy of Russian music touched my heart, just as the amazing circus I saw from the Soviet Union had when it came to China. I was raised to have great respect for Russian artistry in all its forms.

When I saw Elvis Presley perform on television, I thought of Liszt. Liszt was a rock star—he was wild, and women swooned for him. In my imagination he raced motorcycles and flew jet planes faster than the speed of light. Liszt and Monkey King would have gotten along famously. Unlike most of the others, Liszt did not die young. He found a way to live and keep his story going, leaping from one thrilling adventure to another.

I invented adventures for all those composers, just as Monkey King had invented adventures for me. Yet, despite my active mind and my busy fingers, despite my eagerness to learn more music and conquer increasingly difficult pieces, I remained terribly shy at school. I felt different. I *was* different. Except for the children at the Air Force barracks whose parents were musicians themselves, kids saw me as an oddity. I lacked social skills. I spoke awkwardly. Sometimes when I felt uncomfortable among my peers, I would close my eyes to hear the music in my head. My secret fantasy was to avoid school for the rest of my life.

And then came Miss Feng.

She was different. She was young, probably no older than twenty-six or twenty-seven, and she was pretty. She didn't subscribe to the traditional Chinese method of teaching—she was not strict or stern or indifferent. She was sweet and personable, and she rescued me with her kindness. Like Professor Zhu, she entered my life at precisely the right time. Miraculously, Miss Feng managed to turn an extremely introverted six-and-a-half-year-old into an extrovert. She saw that underneath my facade of timidity, I wasn't really timid at all. In fact, I loved people. Miss Feng brought that hidden part of me out into the light of day.

"Lang Lang," she said, "you must not be afraid to speak out your answers. You have a good brain and a strong voice. You must express what you know."

At the time, I didn't want to express anything except my music. I was terrified of sounding stupid in front of the other kids.

"You're a bright boy, Lang Lang," Miss Feng told me. "Let everyone know that."

"I'd rather not say anything," I said.

"You have no choice. When I ask you a question, you'll come to the front of the room, face the class, and respond. You may be uncomfortable at first, but you'll get used to it. You'll do fine."

And she was right. By forcing me to speak up, she showed me that I had nothing to fear. I knew many of the answers and could articulate them well, and my classmates were happy to hear me. The more I did it, the more at ease I felt. If I could play piano in public, I could speak in public as well.

Miss Feng had a three-pronged method of advancing students: if she gave you one stripe, you were the captain of a little team; two stripes, you were in charge of a division (music, math, science, writing); three stripes, you were class leader. I proudly wore two lines on my sleeve because I was the music man. I accompanied our class when we sang, chose the songs, and gave performances for the school. Where other teachers had questioned my leaving early to practice, Miss Feng encouraged it.

She had a deep appreciation of Chinese culture and had us read poems from the Tang dynasty, which took place from A.D. 618 to A.D. 907, a glorious time in our history called the Golden Era, the time of the creation of the Monkey King. We also learned poems from the Sung dynasty, between A.D. 960 and A.D. 1279, verses that conveyed longing and loss. The rhythms of these poems were music to me. They had the same power to lift me up and transport me.

"Everyone has a talent," Miss Feng would say. "It's just a matter of discovering what your special talent happens to be." She would give out extra gold stars to any child who brought in a painting, poem, or something special. If you could run fast or were a skilled gymnast, you'd be similarly rewarded. Miss Feng did not play favorites; every student was showered with attention and affection. And I desperately needed both.

THE YELLOW DOG IS ON THE
WINDOW LEDGE BEHIND ME.

The Yellow Dog

When I was around six and a half, my father left his job at the Air Force orchestra when he was accepted into the Shenyang Police Department as the officer in charge of the entertainment section of the city. He was responsible for keeping out corruption and vice, and he was certainly the right man for the job because he was honest, tough, and afraid of no one. With the position came a new motorcycle and a spiffy uniform. I was proud of him, but I still feared him, perhaps even more because of his uniform. He still never joked or smiled or said much to me except "Practice." When it came to music, he watched me like a hawk, like a policeman ready to punish anything I did that was out of line.

We moved to a simple apartment outside the barracks. My mother, who kept her phone operator job, made sure there were plants and flowers and pretty pictures on the walls, and I had my piano that I played so often and so hard that I broke many pedals and strings. That made playing more challenging, but by then challenges were the very things that kept me going.

"Challenges are there to be met," my maternal grandfather used to tell me.

My great-grandmother and my grandparents were essential to my happiness because they loved me without conditions or restraint. In China, we are taught to respect our elders. Though I didn't have formal instruction in the Chinese version of Buddhism, I do have memories of standing before a holy temple, making wishes on sticks of fire, and burning fake money called *ming jie* on which we'd written the names of family members who had died, to honor their spirits. I was told that those spirits were to be cherished, and I always thought of my grandparents in the same regard, as spirits here on earth to impart wisdom and love.

"Here is where your love of music comes from," said my grandfather one afternoon, pointing at the television as we watched the Beijing Opera.

The opera was spectacular: high, eerie, magical voices, extravagant costumes, acrobatic action, dazzling swordplay, brilliant martial arts. The story was complicated—about historic dynasties and love dramas—and was sung in a local dialect, which we could only understand by reading the subtitles, but he did his best to explain it. I was riveted. Grandfather held me in his arms as we watched together.

"Do you hear how the story goes with the music?" he asked.

I heard the high-pitched voices leaping and then plummeting, then rising again. It sounded like speaking Chinese but in an extremely dramatic way.

"Do you hear how the story drives the music and the music drives the story?"

"I do, Grandpa, I hear everything."

Listening to music with my grandfather gave me confidence that I could meet all challenges and that I wouldn't disappoint my father. I carried within me his faith in me, a different, warmer, less judgmental belief than that of my father.

Sometime after our move, Professor Zhu and my father accompanied me to a series of master classes conducted by American pianists from the Eastman School of Music who were visiting Shenyang. Twelve different artists, twelve separate classes. I attended every one. It was my first time seeing and hearing Westerners play Western classical music, though a month after I began lessons with Professor Zhu, she and I had watched on satellite TV the great Vladimir Horowitz play live from Moscow, his first return to his native country after sixty years. It was also my first time hearing jazz. The average student attending was at least ten years older than I was, but I didn't care. I sat and listened, absorbing the intense emotions each pianist brought to his or her piece. I could feel the joy of Haydn, the lyricism of Schubert, the deep emotion of Brahms. When one of the pianists told the audience, "Remember, it's easy to be a pianist, all you have to do is move your fingers. But to be a *great* pianist, you have to use your mind," I wrote those words down on paper. I was so taken with the event that when it was over, I begged the artists for their autographs. The Chinese translator stopped me. "Leave the artists alone!" he barked. "They do not want to be disturbed!" But an American pianist very politely came over to me, gave me a big smile, and signed his autograph for me.

I look back at myself then and see a child who was much loved, even adored, by his mother, his grandparents, his uncles and aunts. I was gentle in manner, shy, sweet in demeanor, enthusiastic, and curious about the world around me. And yet I was already indoctrinated into China's fiercely competitive system—musicians, painters, mathematicians, virtually anyone who showed signs of talent was ranked. I reveled in competition. Nothing thrilled me more than watching the national Chinese soccer team on television kick the ball deep into their opponent's net. When I won my first competition at age five and was told, for the first time in my life, that I was Number One, I felt invincible—I was the striker who had scored the goal. Now, two years later,

I wanted to score again. Nothing would stand in my way. Winning was everything. For better or worse, that was my nature.

It was exciting, then, when I was seven, not only to enter my second competition but to get on a train and travel from Shenyang to Taiyuan to compete. This was my first trip out of Shenyang, and my father and I took an overnight train to Beijing, where we met up with the other contestants and spent a wondrous day sightseeing and visiting the Great Wall, and then another overnight train to Taiyuan, now a wealthy city but then dusty and dark. During the trip, my father explained the beautiful possibilities that lay ahead.

"Third prize is a television set," he said. "But we don't need one of those, do we?"

"No. We have one."

"Everyone has a television set," said my dad. "Second prize is an electronic piano, but it makes an artificial sound that will throw off your pitch. Electronic pianos have an entirely different touch than real pianos and will lead you in the wrong direction. So you don't want one of those, do you, Lang Lang?"

"No," I said.

"But first prize is a good prize. First prize is the only prize you want."

"What is it?" I asked.

"A new piano. A brand-new *real* piano."

Of course, my father was right. The piano we had gave me no pleasure. My parents had paid five hundred dollars for it, and though it was half of their yearly salary, it was a cheap and inferior instrument with broken pedals and broken strings. I had practiced on it so unmercifully that it was on its last legs. The thought of a new piano excited me. I envisioned its smooth keys and shiny finish. So there I was: a child on a mission. I would not allow success to elude me.

Can a seven-year-old be so determined? I certainly was. My father assured me that victory would be mine, and I embraced his confidence as my own. He gave me a pat on the back before I walked out onstage. I bowed before the judges and began to play.

I had prepared a Mozart, a Czerny, a Bach, and a Chinese piece called "The Brilliant Red Star," which was an appropriate piece because I had every intention of being brilliant.

I played with such fervor, such dazzling theatrics, such generous feeling that I was absolutely certain I had won. I heard the other contestants perform, but I was so into myself that I thought their playing did not equal mine. I already saw the new piano sitting in our apartment back in Shenyang, and I saw myself sitting at the bench, the first-place trophy resting atop the instrument.

When it was time to announce the winners, my dad and I sat in the back of the auditorium. Tension in the room was high. Third place went to a girl, which was a huge relief. Had I won third place, I would have been stuck with the worthless TV. As the judge said, "Second-place prize goes to . . . ," I held my hands to my ears and willed him not to say my name. The tinny sound of that electronic piano would have no place in our home. Another boy's name was called, and I sat up straight, poised to leap out of my seat onto the stage to accept first prize and the warm applause of the crowd.

"The grand prize," said the chief judge, "goes to . . ."

Who?

At first, I thought the man might have just mispronounced my name. But he hadn't. He had announced an entirely different name, the name of a boy who was clearly not me.

I didn't get first place. In fact, I didn't get fourth, fifth, or even sixth. I placed a lowly seventh. It was incomprehensible. I started crying and ran to the judges screaming, "It's not fair! You cheated me!"

My dad had to restrain me. A girl who had also failed to place touched my shoulder and said, "It's okay, we get a consolation prize." The consolation prize was a stuffed yellow dog.

I slapped her hand away. "You played poorly and I didn't. I should have won."

Even as I saw that I was being cruel, my hurt at losing the competition overwhelmed any sympathy I might have felt for her. I was a sore loser, and to this day I feel bad for the way I behaved.

I looked at the toy dog and kicked it. I didn't want a consolation prize. I couldn't, I wouldn't be consoled. But Dad made me retrieve it, and I held it on my lap as we sat silently on the train back to Shenyang. The dog seemed to mock me: it couldn't bark; it couldn't whimper. It just stared at me blankly, reminding me of the devastating moment when I watched someone else receive my shiny new piano.

Professor Zhu understood how devastated I was to lose the contest and tried to give me perspective. "You have a wonderful desire within you to win," she said. "That helps you practice when the nights are cold and the days are warm. But you will not always win. No one does. You will win often, and those victories will be sweet. You will enjoy them. But you must know that the life of an artist is filled with disappointments. They are inevitable. Whether we like them or not, we must live through them."

"The judges weren't fair," I protested.

"What the judges decide is out of our control. True, some judges are unfair. Some have prejudices. Some even have inferior ears or poor taste. But you will learn that most judges will be fair. Most will reward talent. Yet judges, like teachers, are not perfect. We all make mistakes. And at times we will all come across other artists who, for reasons of experience or preparation, will play better than we do. It's a fact we must face. If you fall apart after every contest you fail to win, preparing for the next one will be that much more difficult. You are still a boy, and I understand disappointments are difficult for all boys. But as an artist, you are already a little man. As such, you must learn to face reality. You must absorb that blow, as painful as it is, and still come back strong." Professor Zhu wiped away my tears and kissed my cheeks. In that moment, I loved her with all my heart.

After my failure, I practiced harder than ever. I placed the yellow dog next to the broken pedals of my old piano, and whenever I played a wrong note, I would kick the dog and call it a bad name. It became my whipping boy, suffering for my inadequacies, which I refused to accept. In spite of Professor Zhu's words of wisdom, I was determined never again to lose a contest. If that meant working harder or practicing all night, so be it.

One day I was practicing a Mozart sonata. I had been trying to negotiate an especially difficult passage for several minutes, and as usual when I messed up, I tortured the dog. Suddenly, though, I felt a wave of relaxation wash over me. I don't know where it came from. Just when I was starting to feel myself straining, a sense of surrender overcame me, and, miraculously, I played the piece effortlessly and flawlessly. I looked down at the dog and, for the first time, saw that on his face was a smile. His smile had been there all along, but I hadn't noticed it before.

I had misunderstood that yellow dog. He was not there to torment me or remind me of defeat. He was a source of inspiration. He was there to help, and from that day forward he went from being my torturer to being my friend. Still, as I practiced, I adopted a mantra, sometimes repeated under my breath and sometimes repeated silently; I spoke the two words that never left my consciousness, at least not while I was playing:

Number One, Number One, Number One.

Leaving Home

"You look tired, sweetheart," my mother told me one night after I'd been practicing for a long time. We had eaten dinner at six, and now it was eight. My dad was working and Mom and I were alone.

"Why don't you stop and sit by me?" she asked.

I was glad to do so. My eight-year-old eyes were blurry, my hands hurt, notes were still ringing in my ears.

"Professor Zhu says you are coming along beautifully," said Mom. "She said you are coming along faster than any student she has ever taught."

"Not fast enough," I said.

"Plenty fast. But she's also a little worried."

"About what?" I asked.

"She thinks the musical resources in Shenyang are limited, that you would do far better in Beijing. All the great teachers are there."

"Professor Zhu is a great teacher. I don't want anyone else."

"Professor Zhu *is* a great teacher," my mom agreed. "But what makes her great—and unusual—is that she puts her students first. Most teachers would never even think about giving up a prize student like you. Such a student is what makes a teacher famous, and sometimes rich. Yet Professor Zhu, unlike most instructors, does not accept extravagant gifts from her students' families. Her only concern is that her students realize their potential. And she's convinced that if you want to be known outside China and have an international career, you must first go to Beijing."

"Would we all go—you, Dad, and me?" I couldn't quite imagine how we'd realize Professor Zhu's plans.

"Your father and I are discussing that."

"Could I go with just you, Mom, and let Dad stay here?"

"Those are things we have to work out. But there's nothing to be frightened about," Mom assured me. "Your father and I will protect you. You will always be the most important thing in our lives. We will sacrifice whatever is necessary to ensure your career."

Just then the door opened and Dad walked in.

"Why are you sitting on the couch?" he asked.

"We're talking," Mom answered.

"He should be practicing."

"He has already practiced two hours, Lang Guoren," my mother said.

"Three hours is what we agreed upon," my father fired back.

"I was going to practice the third hour," I said.

"Then stop talking to your mother and start practicing."

"We were talking about something important," I said.

"Nothing is more important than practicing. Now stop the chitchat and get back to the piano."

"You don't understand!" I heard myself screaming. "I want to talk to my mother, and you can't stop me!"

Certainly I was upset at the news about Beijing. And certainly my father might have had a difficult evening at work. But for whatever reason, he flew into a rage, went into the box where I kept my precious Transformers, and started throwing them out the window. I ran to stop him, but he pushed me away.

"Lang Guoren," Mom pleaded, "the boy has done nothing for you to be acting this way."

"He has defied me!"

"Those are mine!" I screamed, grabbing for my toys.

But the louder I screamed, the more Transformers my father flung out the window until they had all landed on the street below. I ran downstairs to retrieve them, but they were broken. Tearfully, I gathered the broken pieces—arms, legs, heads—and put them in a paper bag that I carried upstairs and hid under my bed. Then, with fury, I practiced not for another hour but for two—two hours of miserable practice in which I didn't think about the music I was playing, just my broken Transformers.

My family was in the throes of change, and it wasn't at all clear what form that change would take. Because we lived in a small apartment, I could easily overhear my parents' heated conversations, even when they spoke softly. The subject was always me.

"If he is to become number one in the world," my father told my mother, "we must go to the number one city in China. Beijing is the power city. Beijing is the international city. The Central Conservatory of Music in Beijing is the best in the country. Lang Lang needs the best."

"I explained that to him," I overheard my mother say, "but he was upset. He's afraid of changing teachers."

"He wants to be number one, and he'll do whatever is required."

"He wants me to go with him."

"You know that's impossible, Zhou Xiulan. We need your salary so Lang Lang and I can live in Beijing. I must devote all my time to supervising Lang Lang. The conservatory is not an easy school, but first he has to be accepted, which is even harder. You don't know how competitive those kids and parents are. There are roadblocks everywhere. Beijing is a dangerous place. Our boy needs a man to protect him."

"And you'll give up your job with the police? The position you worked so hard for?"

"I'll have to."

"Have you mentioned this to your parents or your leaders?"

"I have."

"And what do they say?"

"They say I'm crazy."

"And their words do not move you?"

"They don't understand the extent of our son's talent. They see him as a cute little kid who plays the piano well. They don't see that it isn't enough for him to compete in Shenyang. We must compete in Beijing, and then all over the world."

"It will break his heart to be without his mother."

"It will break his heart even more not to achieve his goal," said Dad. "The boy's musical genius must be developed. Everything else is second to that goal."

"Getting into the conservatory won't be easy, Lang Guoren."

"That's just the point. There will be two thousand students from all over China competing to get into the fifth grade," said my father.

"How many will be admitted?"

"About a dozen."

"Do you think Lang Lang will make it?"

"He will if we get to Beijing many months ahead of the entrance exams. Professor Zhu will find us a good teacher in Beijing to rigorously train Lang Lang for those exams. With concentrated effort, he will win admission. He will have to."

"He has never lived without me," said my mother mournfully.

"He will learn to do so. He has no choice. Lang Lang is a little star here in Shenyang, and that's well and good, Zhou Xiulan. But I do not want my son to be a big fish in a little pond. If we stay here, he'll stagnate."

"I don't know if I can live without my son."

"You'll visit."

"It's a twelve-hour train ride."

"You'll come every few months."

"That's not often enough."

"We'll see, Zhou Xiulan. We'll find a way to make it all work. Do you understand?"

"I understand that we must sacrifice for our son. But to live without him is a sacrifice I've never considered."

"For the sake of his future, you must."

There were several seconds of silence. Then my mother said, "I will."

PART TWO

THE

POWER CITY

Fever

I was burning up. My face and arms were covered in sweat. I felt dizzy and confused, sick to my stomach and short of breath.

"We won't leave until you're better," my mother said. "I'll be right here with you."

My father had already gone to Beijing to find a cheap place for us to live, and my mother was supposed to take me there and then return to Shenyang, where her salary would barely support the two households.

Mom patted my forehead with a damp cloth and gave me medicine to calm the fever. But the fever raged on. She slept next to me for two long nights while nightmares had me tossing and turning and waking in fright. In them I was chased by horrible monsters on motorcycles whose arms were poisonous snakes; I was dropped from an airplane into a lake of fire; I was chased through a strange city by a horde of wild rats. No matter how fast I ran or how many times I cried out for my mother, I couldn't escape.

She held me close to her and whispered, "They are just dreams, my darling boy. Nothing bad will happen to you. Your father will always protect you."

"But I want *you!*" I cried.

"I will be there. I will visit. In my heart and mind, you and I will always be together." She seemed to be comforting herself as well, and I knew that her pain was as great as mine.

Then my fever broke.

She packed my things in two suitcases, but she only brought a small one for herself.

On the train to Beijing, I cuddled next to her.

"Remember the time it was cold and snowing and ice was on the ground and I was too lazy to pedal my bicycle and you pushed me through the storm? Remember that, Mom?"

"Of course I remember, sweetheart."

"Were you angry at me for being lazy?"

"You weren't lazy, Lang Lang, you were tired."

"Will my piano arrive in Beijing by the time we get there?" I asked.

"Yes, that's why your father went ahead of us. He's making sure that everything will be in place. Everything will be fine."

But everything didn't feel fine.

The train station in Beijing was ten times the size of any station I had ever seen. I clung to my mother's dress as we made our way through the teeming throngs of people, searching for my father. We looked around for several minutes, but he was nowhere. At once I knew that even though he'd be with me in Beijing, I'd truly be alone.

"The traffic was bad," he said when he finally appeared. "Come, I'll take you to see our new apartment."

He took our bags and led the way to the bus stop. When the bus arrived, it was crowded with people, all talking a mile a minute in strange accents. I couldn't understand a word anyone was saying. No one smiled or acknowledged anyone other than the person they were speaking to. We rode the bus for over an hour. Boulevards a mile wide. Millions of people. Thousands of buildings, hundreds of neighborhoods, all flashing endlessly before my eyes. We finally reached our neighborhood, Feng Tai, a slum that smelled of rancid water and animal urine. The apartment houses were dilapidated, the streets strewn with garbage.

My mother, sensing my despair, whispered in my ear: "As soon as things improve a bit, you'll be able to move to a nice neighborhood."

Our apartment was on the eleventh floor of an ugly building. My father put the key in the lock, opened the door, and said, "There's the piano. Go practice."

"Lang Guoren!" said Mom. "The boy just got off the train. We've been traveling all day."

"He can't afford to miss a day of practice," my father insisted. "He's already missed two days because of the fever. He must practice two hours before going to sleep."

"He's still getting over his sickness," said Mom.

"He's well over it. Don't pamper him. Don't interfere. He needs to practice."

So I practiced.

I played my scales and I played several Liszt études that Professor Zhu had given me as preparation for my meeting with the Beijing teacher she had recommended. I played with tears in my eyes. I played because it was easier to play than not to play; easier to play than to argue with my dad; easier to play than to listen to my parents fight; easier to play than to think about being in Beijing and losing my mother the next morning.

When I awoke, I saw that she had cooked me breakfast.

"Who will cook me breakfast from now on?" I asked her.

"Your father."

"He doesn't know how to cook."

"He will learn."

"I won't eat."

"Yes, you will, darling. You love to eat."

"I won't eat anything he cooks," I said in protest. My father had once cooked for me, and I had thrown up everything I ate because the taste was so disgusting.

My father looked at me from across the room, his face expressionless. He looked at his watch absently. "Next week you meet the new teacher and you're not ready. You and I are staying here. Your mother will go to the station alone."

When my father announced that it was time to go, I ran to my mother and clung to her coat. Her tears only made me feel more desperate. When she was gone and my father demanded that I practice, I poured my heart into my playing. Without my mother to run to, the piano often became an extension of my emotions. It couldn't hold me in its arms the way my mother did, but it was a comfort, a repository for my feelings, and a place to retreat to without angering my father. When I played the piano, I was happy, my father was satisfied, and I felt my mother's presence nearby. When I wasn't playing the piano, I felt that everything was lost.

Professor Angry

I rode on the back of my father's beat-up bike through the streets of Beijing. We were trying to find the Central Conservatory of Music, and we knew the general direction, but we got lost. Later we would learn that the trip normally took an hour. Today it took nearly two.

As we rode through the enormous city, I couldn't help but compare Beijing with Shenyang. In Shenyang, I was known as a brilliant little pianist; my picture had been in the paper. In Beijing, I was nobody. In Shenyang my father was a high-ranking police officer; people feared and respected him. In Beijing he was ignored, just a man riding a third-hand bicycle with a chubby boy on the back. In Shenyang we knew every street, every road and back alley, which we drove through on his police motorcycle. In Beijing we got lost every few minutes. In Shenyang we were in control; in Beijing we were in chaos.

"When you meet this teacher," my father said, "all will be well. She will see your talent and show you how to improve. You will improve enough to win admittance to the conservatory in a year and a half, and from then on you will be taught by the country's great instructors. So it's important to impress this woman. Today you must play perfectly."

I was prepared to play perfectly—if we were going through the misery of living in squalor in Beijing, I was not going to fail. One way or another, I would impress this teacher.

From the moment I met my new teacher, I felt her anger. I had been expecting someone like Professor Zhu, someone who would enjoy my playing and encourage me with praise and support, but Professor Angry—my name for her—was impatient and cold. A short woman with very small hands, she was not in the least impressed with my playing. She never said I had talent or potential. She never said, as most musicians who had heard me before had been saying, that I was extremely advanced for my age, that I played with emotion and technical fire. She never offered me a single compliment. After I played each piece, she would nod and say, "Okay."

In addition to being a teacher, tutoring students hoping to enter the conservatory, she was a professor employed by the conservatory. "That's why it's important," my father said as we left after that first lesson, "that you follow her every instruction. She is the key to getting you in. She knows what the judges want and expect because she is one of the judges."

"But why is she angry with me?"

"That's not anger," my father said, correcting me. "That's professionalism. She has no time to coddle. She's not a mother who pampers a child. She's a high-ranking professor with a job to do. Her job is to challenge you. Your job is to listen to her."

"I don't like her," I said as I got on the back of the bike and we headed into traffic. The afternoon pollution had set in and the air was a dirty shade of brown.

"You don't have to like her," my dad yelled back. "You just have to mind her."

■

My new life in the power city of Beijing consisted of taking lessons from Professor Angry, practicing, and going to elementary school.

I didn't mind the practicing. When Professor Angry gave me difficult pieces to learn, I enjoyed the challenge. If I learned them quickly, I knew I would impress her.

But I never did impress her, or if I did, she never let it show. The only feeling she ever expressed was disappointment.

"Your meter is wrong," she'd say. "Your phrasing is awkward. You don't understand what the composer had in mind."

"You play like a Japanese samurai who killed himself in the end."

"You play like a potato farmer."

"You play like plain water, with no taste. You should be playing like Coca-Cola." Coke had only recently come to China and it was very popular. When I asked her how to make Coca-Cola, the bell would inevitably ring, and she would tell me my lesson was over.

She told me that I played without focus, with no musical sense. During the Cultural Revolution, people threw the great recordings from Horowitz, Rubinstein, and Schnabel out the window and destroyed the scores. She said that I played just like those people, as if I were throwing music out the window, that I had no sense of music making, just crazy fantasies.

I was alarmed by her criticism, but my father wasn't. "This is the real world," he said. "Shenyang was a fairyland. Here teachers don't mince words. She's tough, and that's good. That's what you require." In fact, I later learned that Professor Angry had been taught in just the same way by her piano teacher.

The mild weather soon turned bitter cold. There was no heating in our apartment—none at all. We were living on the money my mother was sending from Shenyang, $150 a month, but that was barely enough to pay the rent, pay for lessons, and buy vegetables, eggs, and an occasional piece of chicken. There was no money to buy even a small space heater, and of course a TV was out of the question. When I practiced, my father bundled me up in layers of clothing. I would wear two pairs of pants and two shirts. The heat of my playing kept my hands warm. In fact, I would play long into the night to keep from having to climb into a bed that was so cold I couldn't sleep. Wanting to be sure I got a good night's rest, my father would get in the bed before me to warm it up.

But my late-night practicing was more than just a survival tactic. It was a compulsion for me as well as for my father. "If you practice more," he repeated, "you will finally please the teacher. You must please this teacher at all costs." I couldn't stand the idea of not living up to her expectations. If that meant working harder, so be it. But I also couldn't stand the idea of pleasing this teacher who never thought I was any good.

At first I practiced after dinner until 7:00. Then until 8:00. Then until 9:00, 10:00, sometimes even 11:00. The walls of the apartment building were thin, and neighbors on all sides—even those from adjoining buildings—began complaining.

"Stop the racket!"

"That music is driving us crazy!"

"I'll kill you if you don't stop!"

"I'll break your hands!"

"I'll call the cops!"

"Ignore them," my father would say flatly. "Keep practicing."

If they persisted in complaining, he'd answer them with screams of his own. "My boy is a genius! You are lucky to get to hear him play for free! One day people will pay good money for the privilege!"

Eventually someone did call the cops. One night there was a big bang on the door. "Police!" a voice bellowed. "Open up!" Two stern-faced officers barged in, as if to apprehend a couple of criminals.

"Where's your local work permit?" they asked my father. "Where is your resident permit for Beijing?"

My father didn't have a work permit. His only job was making sure I got into the music conservatory. And we didn't have enough money for resident papers. He admitted that he was without papers.

"That's a serious violation," they said. "Besides that, there's a code that prohibits excessive noise after 8:00 p.m."

I was frightened. Would they send us back to Shenyang?

"Look, guys," my father finally said. "I was a police officer. I headed up the vice squad in Shenyang. Here is my uniform, and here are my official papers." He showed both to the policemen as he kept talking. "I know how tough it is to be a cop, and I know you guys are just doing your job. But this is an exceptional situation. My son is a genius and on the brink of greatness. Here are several articles written about him in the Shenyang newspaper."

My dad kept those articles on him at all times. The cops read them carefully and compared the picture of the boy in the newspaper with me. They could see my father wasn't lying. "I gave up my work to dedicate my life to my son and his talent," my father continued. "We live off my wife's modest salary. She had to stay behind to support us. Financially, we are in dire straits. All we have is little Lang Lang's willingness to practice day and night. He must. Two thousand students will audition for the conservatory, but only twelve will be admitted. We are determined that he will be among the twelve. We are determined he will be Number One, and you can help us. In this case, help just means letting us be. We are honest, hardworking people. Please understand."

My father spoke with such eloquence and passion that the policemen turned from stern to sympathetic. They both patted me on the top of my head and told my father that he was right, that he was a good dad with a good son, and that the city of Beijing needed more citizens like us.

"Good luck," they said to me before leaving. "We hope you win admission to the conservatory."

■

My father may have been a great debater, but he was a lousy cook. He overcooked vegetables and even had a hard time making rice. Eating his tasteless meals made me miss my mother even more. Back home, she had made delicious dumplings or pork or fresh fish every evening. With my father, there was no joy in cooking or eating. We saved money by buying cheap food, and my mother did the same in Shenyang, spending less than ten dollars a month on food for herself.

At that time, the neighborhood of Feng Tai was on the city line of Beijing, out in the middle of nowhere. I missed my friend Mark Ma and my schoolmates from Miss Feng's class. There were other music students from Shenyang who had also moved to Beijing and had won admission to the conservatory—older children who were living with their mothers—but they were strangely distant and cold to me and my father.

"Why aren't they being nice?" I asked my father.

"I don't know," he said. "Maybe they are jealous of you. Maybe they think you will make them look bad."

"But they were so friendly back in Shenyang."

"Beijing is not Shenyang. Beijing changes people. Don't worry about them. Just worry about practicing. You aren't practicing enough."

So I practiced even more.

And at elementary school, kids who themselves were from the sticks—we lived so far from the center of Beijing that the neighborhood could hardly be called sophisticated—made fun of my accent, calling me "Little Farmer from the North." "Oh, the farmer plays piano," they would taunt me. "What kind of sound do you think he can make?"

Professor Angry had given me one of the difficult Beethoven variations to play. "Phrase it delicately," she told me. "Don't play it heavy-handedly." I welcomed her direction. I took up the challenge. I tackled the piece enthusiastically. I practiced it until my fingers ached, until I thought I had mastered it. As I rode to my lesson on the back of my dad's rickety bike through the pouring rain, I heard the piece inside my head. The notes rang out. My fingers motionlessly danced over an invisible keyboard. I didn't see the bicycles, cars, and buses; I didn't see the traffic lights and the throngs of pedestrians. I saw Beethoven's story about finding one's way through a complex maze. When we arrived at Professor Angry's studio, she hardly looked at me. She seemed nervous and, as always, impatient.

"Begin," she said.

After a few minutes she stopped me, saying, "You're playing this piece like you're afraid of it. You're playing too lightly."

"You said to play it delicately," I reminded her.

"No, I didn't."

She had, and I wanted to remind her again, but I was a little boy and she was a distinguished teacher. I held my tongue.

I continued playing.

"Too light," she said. "Too tentative. You must approach this with a heavier hand."

"But, Professor—" I began to say.

She cut me off. "No 'buts' about it. You must pay attention to my directions or I can no longer teach you."

Her threat frightened me.

"If this piece is too challenging, I can give you something easier."

My father broke in and said, "Lang Lang doesn't want anything easier. He wants something harder."

"You," said the teacher, "how can I give him something harder if he comes here unprepared?"

"He will never again come here unprepared," my father promised.

But I'm not unprepared, I thought. *I know this piece. I can play this piece. I know every note. Professor Angry gave me one set of instructions, and then changed her mind when I followed them. Now she is not telling the truth. She is a liar.*

"She is your teacher, and she is the only way you're getting into the conservatory!" my father screamed at me as we approached the stand where he had locked his bicycle.

"But she's crazy!" I said. "She tells me how to play a piece, and I learn it that way. Then, when I follow her instructions, she scolds me and says play it another way."

I got on the back of the bike, and my father, still enraged, headed out into traffic. Only this time he was not in the bicycle lane but in the car lane. His anger was causing him to lose his good sense. Cars sped past on either side of us, their drivers shouting and honking.

"You're so stupid!" my father yelled, ignoring the cars that were practically sideswiping us. "You're so lazy! You aren't listening to the teacher, and you aren't playing what she wants to hear!"

My father steered the bike erratically. I had my arms around his waist, but it was difficult to hold on.

"You are ruining your chance for success! You are being stubborn by playing the way *you* want to play—and defying the teacher!"

"I'm not!" I screamed back, tears streaming down my face, the wind biting my eyes. "I'm trying!"

"You're not trying hard enough!"

"I can't try any harder!"

"Then you are a fool and an idiot!"

With that, he jerked the handlebars of the bike to the right to avoid a truck. The move was so sudden that I lost my grip and started falling to the street. I was terrified. If I fell, I'd smash my head on the concrete and a car would run me over. My father, feeling my hands slipping away, yelled, "Hang on!"

I grabbed the sleeve of his jacket. I was half on and half off the bike, my body dangling inches from the street. Just when I felt myself slipping off completely, my dad managed to catch me. While still ped-aling, he brought me back up with his right hand and held on until I was able to steady myself, but he continued to ride in the car lane and, under his breath, still spoke of how poorly I had performed for the exalted professor.

That night I practiced the piece according to my new directions. I knew I had no choice, but I also knew that I was dealing with a teacher who wouldn't be happy with me no matter what I did. When I returned to her studio a week later and played the Beethoven with more force, she shook her head.

"Something is still missing," she said.

"What?" I wanted to know.

She didn't have an answer for me.

"You're not listening to me!" she shouted.

"I'm trying," I said helplessly.

"Don't talk back to the professor!" my father screamed.

I fought back tears, and because I was so upset, I made several mistakes when I played the piece again.

My father was furious. That night he threw a hard leather shoe at me. The anger behind his action hurt even more than the blow.

"You are letting us all down," he said. "You are letting down your mother, you are letting me down, you are letting down yourself! You are bringing shame on your family!"

His accusations against me got wilder. He had never talked to me this way before. He'd had no need to. I was a star pupil in Shenyang, but in Beijing I had lost my shine, and the more Professor Angry criticized me, the crazier my father became. Deep down, he may have detected the inconsistency of her critiques, but because he was a man who respected authority implicitly, he wasn't prepared to challenge her. I felt hopeless and filled with despair.

Things have to get better, I thought to myself. But they only got worse.

Shame

My mother came to visit, but for only two days, during which time she cleaned my father's and my messes and did our laundry. She brought us fruit and pork from Shenyang as if she had come to feed refugees. During her visit, I never let her out of my sight. When she cooked my favorite meals, I felt a million times better. When she listened to me practice and told me I was playing better than ever, I embraced her with all my strength. Encouragement was something I hadn't felt in months. Like her wonderful cooking, her encouragement gave me the nourishment I'd been missing.

The weather had turned mild then, and when I wasn't practicing, she and I took walks along the great boulevards of Beijing. She thought it was important that I get out of the house more. During our walks I told her about Professor Angry. But my mother couldn't understand how someone could not like my playing.

"Maybe that's her way of motivating you," she suggested.

I also told my mother something I had not dared to mention to my father. I had become friendly with a girl who also studied with Professor Angry. Sometimes I would help her practice, show her techniques and exercises. One day the girl told me that Professor Angry had told her that she didn't think I had talent. The girl also told me that our friends from Shenyang who were studying at the conservatory were saying bad things about me and my father.

My mother was silent for a while. We stopped at a small park and sat under the shade of a tree. "People are complicated, Lang Lang," she finally said. "People can be helpful and people can be harmful. Some don't like to see others succeed. There's nothing we can do about that. We live our lives in spite of them. We go on and accomplish our goals. We ignore them."

"I know, Mom," I told her, "but I can't ignore Professor Angry. And I can't do anything she likes. I'm afraid she'll drop me as a student, and then how will I get into the conservatory?"

"Your father thinks she's a good instructor, sweetheart. He knows music and says she is among the best. I know she's very demanding, but as long as you keep practicing and improving, everything will be fine. I promise you." She bent over to hug me and kiss my cheek.

Then I asked my mother if she could buy me a new Transformer. I'd been passing by a toy store for weeks and studying all the Transformers in the window, and I knew just the one I wanted.

"Then let's go, darling. Let's get you a treat."

Mom's visit was short-lived, and when she left, she took the mild weather with her. All that remained was the anxiety of facing my weekly lessons. Even when I was absolutely convinced that I had mastered a difficult Schubert or Tchaikovsky piece, Professor Angry sat there unimpressed. My fingers flew over the keys; my command of the technical challenges was good; I played with the appropriate emotions. At home, even my father had to admit that I was playing well. And yet Professor Angry was never satisfied.

"Something's missing," she would complain, but she never said what.

My frustration mounted. Dad stopped saying that I wasn't practicing enough, because it was clear I was. He was in the apartment, watching over me, supervising my every move. He knew something was wrong.

Dad and I had to ride through a thunderstorm and sandstorm to get to Professor Angry's studio. In the spring, strong winds blow dirty yellow sand from the Gobi desert all the way to Beijing, and we would get covered with it. When it rained, the rain would plaster the dust to our faces and clothes. Though I wore my yellow rain hood, every time the bike hit a puddle, I'd get splattered in the face with muddy water. By the time we arrived, I was drenched and dirty, and so was my father. We were shivering from the cold, but Professor Angry did not offer us towels.

"If you'd let us dry off, Professor," said my dad, "Lang Lang can get started playing for you."

"That won't be necessary," she said in a voice colder than ice.

"Why not?" asked my dad.

"I've decided to no longer train your son."

Dead silence.

I felt tears welling in my eyes. I saw my father's eyes turn red.

"I don't understand," he said. "My son is a genius."

"Most parents of young pianists consider their progeny geniuses. The overwhelming majority of these children are not. Not only is your son far from a genius, Lang Guoren, he does not have the talent to win admission to the conservatory. I'm afraid he is a lost cause."

"But, Professor," my father argued, "he has won competitions. Articles have been written about him. In Shenyang he is famous."

"Shenyang is not Beijing."

"You must reconsider, Professor. We are betting everything on this boy's talent. I left a good job to live in a hovel just so you could train him."

"I am sorry, Lang Guoren, but my mind is made up. Now if you'll excuse me . . ."

Still dripping wet, we went back out into the rain. Holding on to my father's waist, riding back to our apartment, I couldn't stop crying. My life as a musician was ruined. My future had collapsed. When my father got off the bike, I couldn't tell if his face was covered with raindrops or tears. It didn't matter. Nothing mattered anymore.

My father was spinning out of control. For the first time in my life, I sensed that he didn't know what to do. He didn't know how to handle the fact that I had no teacher and no way to prepare for the conservatory audition. We were strangers in the vast, heartless city, lost and without resources.

My only consolation was the school choir at the elementary school I was attending. The choir's conductor had asked me to accompany the singers on the piano, and I loved doing so because the kids praised my playing. The pianist I had replaced had often made mistakes, but I made very few; during an otherwise miserable time in my life, when I felt unappreciated and untalented, the choir was my one saving grace.

On the morning after Professor Angry rejected me, my father woke me up an hour early.

"I want you to practice an extra hour before school," he said, "and an extra hour after school. When you get home at 3:00, practice not until 5:00 but until 6:00."

I didn't see the point. Whom was I practicing for? But my father was in no mood to be questioned; there was a crazy look in his eyes I hadn't seen before.

"You must practice like there's no tomorrow," he said. "You must practice until everyone sees that they cannot reject you, that you are Number One and will always be Number One."

That day at choir practice I tried to forget Professor Angry and my dad's insane mood. The teacher had kind words to say about me, but she felt that the choir needed more work and extended the rehearsal for an extra ninety minutes. I knew my father would be upset that I couldn't start practicing at 3:00, but I had no choice. I figured that once I told him that I had, in fact, been playing the piano, he'd calm down.

After the rehearsal, I walked home quickly. As I approached our building, I could see my father leaning over the balcony of our eleventh-story apartment. He was screaming at me at the top of his lungs.

"Where have you been? You are late! You can't be trusted! You have ruined your life! You've ruined all our lives!" His voice was wildly shrill. My dad had screamed at me before, but not like this. He sounded as though he was truly out of his mind. And when I walked inside the apartment, his assault was even worse.

"You've missed nearly two hours of practicing, and you can never get them back!" he yelled. "It's too late to make up that time! It's too late for everything! Everything is ruined!"

"It's not my fault," I said. "The teacher asked us to stay late to practice—"

"I don't believe you."

"I'm telling you the truth, Dad. I'm—"

"You're a liar and you're lazy! You are horrible. And you have no reason to live. No reason at all!"

"What are you talking about?"

"You can't go back to Shenyang in shame!" he cried out. "Everyone will know you were not admitted to the conservatory! Everyone will know this teacher has fired you! Dying is the only way out!" I started backing away from my father. His screaming only got louder, more hysterical. "I gave up my job for you! I gave up my life! Your mother works and starves for you, everyone depends on you, and you're late, you're fired by this teacher, you're not practicing, and you don't do what I tell you to do. There's no reason for you to live. Only death will solve this problem. Die now rather than live in shame! It will be better for both of us. First you die, then I die."

For the first time in my life, I felt a deep hatred for my father. I began cursing him.

"Take these pills!" he said, handing me a bottle of pills I later learned were strong antibiotics. "Swallow all thirty pills right now. Everything will be over and you will be dead!"

I ran out onto the balcony to get away from him.

"If you won't take the pills," he screamed, "then jump! Jump off right now! Jump off and die!"

He came after me, and I started kicking him hard. I had never behaved so violently before, but I was afraid he would throw me off the balcony; at that moment, I felt he might do anything. I imagined myself falling eleven floors, my skull crushed against the pavement, my blood, my life spilling out of me.

"Stop!" I begged. "You're crazy! Leave me alone! I don't want to die! I'm not going to die!" I ran back into the apartment.

"If you won't jump," my father yelled, "then swallow these pills! Swallow every last one!"

My whole life my father had taught me to protect my hands at all costs; they were the most precious parts of my body. But now I started hammering the wall with my fists. I would pulverize my hands, break every bone. I beat the walls like a fighter punching his opponent in the face.

"Stop!" my father screamed.

"No!" I screamed back.

"You'll ruin your hands!"

"I hate my hands, I hate you, I hate the piano. If it weren't for the piano, none of this would have happened! The piano is making you crazy! The piano is making you want to kill me! I hate everything!"

"Stop!" my father screeched.

He ran over and hugged me, now sobbing. "Stop," he kept saying as he pulled me to his chest. "I'm sorry," he said, "I'm sorry, I'm so sorry, but you can't hurt your hands. Please, Lang Lang, don't hurt your hands. I don't want you to die, my son. I just want you to practice."

"I hate you," I said through my tears. "I'll never practice again. I'll never touch the piano for as long as I live."

Uncle No. 2

*N*ever practice the piano.

Never play the piano.

Never even look at the piano.

Never speak to my father.

Never even look at my father.

Never forgive him.

Never stop hating him. Hate him every hour, every minute, every second. Hate him for wanting me to die. Hate him for not believing me when I told him that it was the teacher who made me late. Hate him for not believing Professor Angry was a liar. Hate him for making me hate the piano because I had always loved it, ever since I can remember, ever since I saw Tom chasing Jerry across the keys, ever since I first heard the beautiful notes, the beautiful melodies, the chords and the harmonies and the magic of music.

All that is gone.

Now there is no beauty. No music. Now there is nothing.

Now I'm just a kid without a dream going to school in a strange city, living with a father I hate.

■

I couldn't even look at my father. When he cooked tasteless vegetables for me at night, I turned my back to him as I ate. When he asked me questions, I didn't answer. He was ashamed of himself for what he had done, and walked around mostly in silence, but I didn't care. His apologies meant nothing to me. I couldn't forgive him.

Sometimes he would say, "You need to start practicing again, Lang Lang. You're wasting time and forgetting everything you've learned." But his voice had lost its authority. He knew he couldn't force me to practice; he was too guilty, too humiliated for having lost his senses.

"You'll play again," my father would say. "You'll have to. The piano is part of your soul." But I no longer had the urge to play. I had even stopped accompanying the school choir, the one thing that had given me pleasure since our move to Beijing.

If I had been older and braver, I would have run away; I would have hitchhiked back to Shenyang to live with my mother. But I didn't know the way, and I lacked the courage. Besides, I was only nine years old. I cried myself to sleep every night.

"Why won't you play?" asked the choir conductor at my elementary school.

"My father—" I started to say.

"Go on," my teacher urged me.

"Oh, it's nothing," I said.

"It has to be something," she insisted. "One day you were playing brilliantly for our choir, and the next day you stopped. What happened?"

I wanted to tell her everything. But I was ashamed of having such a crazy father, and I couldn't tell her how he wanted me to jump off the balcony and kill myself with pills, because she was the teacher who had kept me late. I didn't want her to think it was her fault. So I kept quiet, and when I got home that night, I threw down my schoolbooks and cried.

"Will you start practicing again today?" my father begged pathetically.

I didn't bother to answer him.

Weeks went by. A month, then two, then three.

I couldn't call my mother, because we didn't have a phone. I desperately wanted her to come visit, but she couldn't get away from work. I even more desperately wanted her to take me away from my father, but he told me that would never happen. Then what *would* happen? What was the point of staying here in Beijing if I wasn't going to play the piano and I wasn't even going to apply to the conservatory? What was the point of living?

I became depressed. Maybe my father had been right. Maybe dying was better. By now I was missing the piano—life without music made no sense. I would hear music in my mind and felt desperate to play; playing often seemed like the only thing that could comfort me. But I still couldn't get myself to sit down at the piano bench. The thought of practicing brought back fresh memories of my father brutalizing me. Besides, playing the piano would have pleased my father. I wanted to torture him.

I was stuck in hell.

Spring turned to summer, and because I wasn't practicing, I had time on my hands. I'd go out for walks by myself. Sometimes I'd stop at a fruit and vegetable market and buy a peach or a pear with the little change my father left me. One day in June I walked through the market, stopped at a cart of watermelons, and began tapping one to test its ripeness.

"You have a different touch," said the fruit vendor. "Most people poke the melon. But you treat it like it's a musical instrument."

"I used to play piano."

"Used to?" asked the man. "You look awfully young to have already retired."

"I don't play anymore," I responded.

"That's too bad. I would imagine you were very good."

"I had a teacher who said I wasn't talented."

"Well, teachers are just human beings like the rest of us," said the watermelon man. "They make mistakes. What's your name?"

"Lang Lang."

"A beautiful name!"

"What's your name?" I asked.

"Han."

Han was younger than my father, solidly built from his years of training in kung fu, and dark-skinned from his years of working in the fields as a farmer. He had warm, honest eyes. Later I learned that he was from a family of farmers and had left his wife and son, who was around my age, in the countryside to come to Beijing with his brother to make a living. Because he was so kind, I opened up to him. I told him the dishes that my mother used to make, that she lived back in Shenyang. In fact, because I needed to talk, I told him our whole story.

"You must be a very great piano player," he said when I was through. "For your father and mother to make such sacrifices must mean that they believe you will be Number One."

"I am Number Zero," I said. "I don't even have a number anymore."

"I believe you'll be Number One," Han insisted. "Right now you are just feeling sad. From time to time we all feel sad. But I think this huge watermelon will cheer you up. When you eat it, I want you to think happy thoughts."

When I told Han that I didn't have the money to buy an entire watermelon, he told me that it was not for sale.

"I was saving it as a gift for a great musician," he told me. "This is your reward for having practiced so long and hard. This is your prize."

"But you've never heard me play."

"I have heard you in my imagination, and my imagination is very rich. Take this watermelon with my regards, and tell your father he has a son to be proud of," he said.

When I walked into our apartment with the watermelon, I spoke to my father for the first time since our fight. I had to tell him about Han.

"He sounds like a nice man," my father said. "I'll have to buy my vegetables from him."

The next day my father came home with a shopping bag filled with produce. "I told Han that I was your father," said Dad, "and he treated me like an important leader. He gave me his best vegetables at a discount price. You're right, Lang Lang, he's a great guy!"

Within the week, my father invited Han to our small apartment. Han cooked a delicious meal for us and, just like that, became part of our family. I called him Uncle No. 2. His easygoing personality relieved much of the tension between me and my father. With Han around, I didn't feel angry. Finally my dad had someone he could talk to, and so did I.

Yet for all the goodwill that Han created, I remained adamant about not practicing. When Han asked me to give a small recital just for him, I said, "Uncle No. 2, I'd love to show you how I play, but I'm no longer a pianist. I'm just a regular kid."

"I understand," he said. "I am a patient man and I will wait until you are ready."

"I will never be ready."

"Lang Lang, my boy," he said, "never is a long, long time."

Another three or four weeks passed. Han came by often, and often asked me to play, but I refused. When I looked at the scores sitting atop the piano, I could see holes where mice had chewed into the paper. Each leaf was covered in a fine layer of dust.

Then, in a strange twist of fate, a neighbor came by, a man who had bitterly complained about the racket my music made—in fact, of all the neighbors, he had complained most. Once, when I'd been pounding the piano late into the night, he had thrown stones at our window. He was the guy who had called the cops.

"What's wrong now?" my father asked the neighbor as he stood in our doorway. "It can't be the noise. My son no longer plays."

"That's why I'm here."

"I don't understand," said my dad.

"His playing helped me."

"I thought his playing drove you crazy."

"I thought so too. I had a disease of the nerves. The doctor gave me herbs to treat the disorder, and I thought your kid's playing made it worse. So I screamed at him and complained to the authorities. I even threw pebbles at your window."

"I know," my father said. "Once you broke the glass, and I had to pay to have it replaced."

"I will pay you back. I need your son to start playing the piano again."

"What? That doesn't make sense. His playing bothered your nerves."

"It turns out that it *helped* my nerves. I'd complain and complain for him to stop, but he never would. After a while, though, his playing—his beautiful playing, I must add—did something to me. The music calmed me. My unsteady hands stopped shaking. I felt less jumpy. Since he's stopped, the bad nerves have returned. I'm shaking worse than ever. I need for him to play."

"Maybe you can buy a record," I suggested from across the apartment.

"I can't afford a stereo system," said the neighbor. "But your playing is free. Your playing is a gift to all of us. May I ask why you stopped?"

My father began to explain but stopped himself. Finally he said, "Lang Lang will tell you why."

I tried, but I couldn't. The story was too painful.

A Return to Music

Dear Lang Lang,

We miss you very much when we rehearse. Some of the other kids are playing the piano, but they do not play as well as you do.

We hope we did not do anything to hurt your feelings. If we did, it was not on purpose and we apologize. You play beautifully and your playing makes us want to sing beautifully. We are sending you a little gift to let you know we want you to come back.

Your friends,
The Chorus

The note was signed by every kid in the class, and along with it came the newest Transformer. The kids knew that I loved them.

I didn't tell my dad about the note or the gift. I told Han.

"You must be really popular for your schoolmates to beg you to come back," said Han.

"It's not me," I said, "it's my playing."

"Well, son, you *are* your playing."

"Uncle No. 2," I said, "do you think I should start playing again?"

"Only if you want to. Do you want to?"

"I don't want to make my father happy."

"I can see why you're mad at your father," said Han. "But being mad at the piano is a different thing. The piano didn't hurt you. You love the piano. When you play, you bring out love in other people. Even your classmates."

I told Han I would consider accompanying the choir again on the condition that he wouldn't tell my father. I still wanted to make my father miserable, and I was afraid that if he knew I had gone back to the piano, he'd go crazy all over again and would want me to practice twenty straight hours or jump off the balcony. Han promised not to reveal my secret.

I hadn't played the piano in four months. I still hadn't decided whether to accompany the chorus, but I figured it couldn't hurt to walk past the room where they were rehearsing for a school competition. I told myself I didn't have to go in if I didn't want to, but as I passed the doorway, one of the singers saw me.

"Lang Lang!" she exclaimed. "You've come back to play for us!"

I began to explain that I wasn't sure, but my schoolmate was too excited to listen.

"Lang Lang's back!" she shouted. "Lang Lang's back!" They explained that without me accompanying them, they'd never win the competition. There was no one in that provincial school who could accompany them at all.

The other kids ran out into the hallway and surrounded me. One very nice boy, whom I'll never forget, was a stutterer. "La-la-la-la-la-lang-lang is b-b-b-ack," he cried out. They took me by the hand, led me to the piano, and handed me the second movement of Mozart's Sonata in C major, K. 330. What could I do? When my fingers touched the keys, I immediately felt a thrill. The weight of my anger—all my resentment and frustration—lifted, and suddenly I was floating on a breeze of Mozart's music. With the kids gathered around me, I didn't want to stop playing. The bitter Lang Lang was gone, and so was the memory of Professor Angry. For the first time in months, I was smiling. When I finally lifted my hands from the keyboard, my schoolmates applauded and called for more.

That afternoon the choir and I rehearsed for an extra hour. When I arrived home, my father didn't say a word about my tardiness. And though I was elated, I didn't share that happiness with him. I couldn't. I still hated him.

If I was alone in the apartment, I would play a small piece, say, by Haydn, just to lift my spirits. But the moment I sensed Dad approaching, I stopped. If he asked me, "Did I hear you playing, Lang Lang?" I simply wouldn't answer, knowing that my silence added to his misery.

"When will you start playing?" he asked.

Still I said nothing.

"I want you to answer me, Lang Lang!" he screamed.

I turned my back on him.

Then something of a miracle occurred. Maybe "miracle" is too strong a word, but at the time it felt like nothing less.

I was walking home from school, wanting to buy the newest *Dragon Ball Z* comic book, but I had no money. I considered going by Uncle No. 2's fruit and vegetable stand to borrow some, but Han had given us so much that asking for comic book money felt greedy. I went straight home instead.

Walking down the hallway to our apartment, I thought I heard a familiar voice. The closer I got to our door, the more certain I was. I could hardly believe it. Standing in our apartment was Professor Zhu, talking to my dad. I embraced her, tears running down my cheeks. She had recently returned to China from a year in Dallas, Texas, where she had been a visiting professor, spending time with her daughter, who lived there; as soon as she had come back, she had contacted my father, who had been trying to reach her. My first words to her were to ask her if I had talent.

"Of course you do."

"But the teacher fired me. She said I'm a terrible pianist."

"She has made a serious mistake, Lang Lang. Soon she will see the gravity of it. Now that I am back, we will find you another teacher."

"Here at the conservatory?"

"Yes, of course."

"And a new teacher will accept me even though I was fired by Professor Angry?"

Professor Zhu told me she had already spoken to a couple, Zhao Ping-Guo, a prominent professor of the piano, and his famous wife, Professor Ling, the head of the piano department, and they were eager to hear me play. She told me that I would play for both of them, and they would decide which one of them would be my teacher. And she offered to give me some lessons to get me in shape for the audition. I sat down at the piano and began to play for her. I felt I played beautifully, and so did Professor Zhu. She praised and encouraged me as she had always done, and it felt good to be with someone who taught with love. I had forgotten the feeling.

That night Professor Zhu joined us for dinner. After another long lesson, I grew tired, but when I climbed into bed and closed my eyes, sleep didn't come immediately. I was too excited. As I was reviewing the events of the day, I overheard my father and Professor Zhu speaking. My father was saying things he had never told me.

"Tell me, what do you think happened?" my teacher asked Dad. "Why did this woman reject Lang Lang? Surely it wasn't because he lacked talent."

"She was fed rumors about me that, unfortunately, she began to believe."

"What kinds of rumors?"

"That I was connected to criminals. That I have a history of foul play back in Shenyang."

"But you were a policeman in Shenyang. You were fighting criminals, not consorting with them. All she had to do was check the facts."

"Of course. But she never bothered to."

"Who was spreading these rumors?"

"Pianist friends from Shenyang."

"I'd hardly call them friends," said Professor Zhu.

"Former friends," said my father. "Jealous people who realized that if Lang Lang were admitted to the conservatory, he would immediately become the star attraction."

Professor Zhu told my father to listen to her carefully. She told him that she was sure that Professor Zhao or Professor Ling would take me on as a student, and she fully expected I would be accepted into the conservatory. "But you must understand, Lang Guoren," she told him, "given the enormity of Lang Lang's talent, the challenges will not end there. Others will continue to be jealous of him—and not only students, but competitive teachers as well. In an ideal world, the academy would be free from petty envy, but it is not. Wealthy parents are at a great advantage because they can buy a teacher's favor—or, during competitions, even a judge's favor. But you have only your tenacity and desire to protect your son. You must closely monitor everything that happens at the conservatory and make certain Lang Lang's studies are not compromised."

"I have every intention of doing just that."

"Alone," said my teacher, "I'm not sure Lang Lang can find his way through the maze, but with you by his side he has a fighting chance."

"I'm there," said my father. "I'm by my son's side. Nothing and no one can push me away."

Nine Months

It was fall, and my audition for the conservatory was in the summer. I had nine months to prepare with my new teacher, Professor Zhao. My father had taken me to audition for him and his wife on the wrong date, and when we'd arrived, Professor Zhao happened to be there, working with another student. The couple had waited all of the previous afternoon for me, but he was willing to listen to me play when he finished up with his student, and after I played, he agreed to take me on.

We had heard that more students than ever were applying to the conservatory that year, as many as three thousand. Only a dozen would be accepted. And yet my father would only be satisfied if I placed first among all the applicants. "Short of that," he insisted, "there is no victory."

I took my father's words to heart. He and I had reconciled. It was not an easy or complete reconciliation but a necessary one. Part of me couldn't stop hating him for what he had done to me, but another part of me acknowledged a fact that I could not change: I wanted what he wanted. I wanted to be Number One. I wanted to win over the best teachers in the best schools so I could enter competitions and win every last one of them. For all the differences in our personalities, my father and I shared an obsession. His drive was great, but so was mine, and I knew that I needed him.

Though we didn't exchange words, my dad and I had a new understanding. We had survived one teacher, and now, thanks to Professor Zhu, we had a new one, one with knowledge and influence. Whereas Professor Zhao's wife was strict and intimidating, and I was glad she was not my teacher, Professor Zhao was much mellower. He had studied in Russia and was steeped in the music and teaching methods of that culture. He was a handsome man, with carefully coiffed hair, like the host of a television show, and he dressed elegantly, cutting a dashing figure. His easygoing manner suited me well. He spoke softly and never threatened. When I went to him for my Tuesday lessons, his main criticism was that I was too uptight. "Right now, with your strong technique, you are chasing the music. That will never work. You must let the music come to you. You must let the music come *through* you. Don't hold in your breath. Breathe naturally. Lower your arms when you play. Try to take it easy."

"Take it easy" was a difficult concept for me to grasp. "Easy" wasn't part of my approach to music. I liked difficult pieces. The more difficult pieces I learned, the more contests I'd win. So what did "easy" mean?

Professor Zhao explained that just as breathing comes naturally, playing the piano came naturally to me. Just as if I became overly conscious of the act of breathing, I would interfere with the natural flow of my breath, if I became overly conscious of the act of playing, I would interfere with my natural instincts and ability. "It is a matter of allowing yourself to feel a flow that is both inside the music and inside you," he told me.

Try not to try, I kept telling myself. And little by little, I got the idea.

■

My father was trying. He'd seen his terrible mistake, and in his way he tried to make up for his moment of madness. Though he still never smiled, and still would call me lazy, he seemed to understand that our relationship couldn't focus solely on the piano. One afternoon he found two Ping-Pong paddles and a ball, and we spent an hour or so hitting the ball against our own apartment's uneven brick wall, chasing it as it bounced around the room.

"I see you practicing very hard for your lessons with Professor Zhao," he said. "After two or three hours, it's a good idea to rest. We'll play Ping-Pong during your break. That way you can go back to practicing for even longer."

Ping-Pong helped ease the tension between us, as did the arrival of Lang Yifeng, my cousin.

My dad's brother's son, Yifeng, who was just six months younger than I was, had come from Shenyang to live with us because he, too, had great musical talent as a clarinetist. When he arrived, I couldn't have been happier. It was like having a brother. We had many interests in common, and, like any siblings, we also had great differences.

Yifeng, at age ten, was already acting like a teenager. He loved to party, hated practicing, and did everything he could to avoid it. His friends were other woodwind and brass players, and they didn't have to work half as hard as the pianists or the violinists—at least that's how I saw it. And because Yifeng was under my dad's care, he took some of the pressure of Dad's discipline off me. I was the good, dutiful student, and Yifeng was the indifferent one. The more my father screamed at Yifeng, the less he screamed at me. How could anyone call me lazy when Yifeng slacked off all the time?

But while my cousin's arrival changed the dynamics of our household considerably, one thing did not change: my determination to gain admission to the conservatory.

When the weather was brutally hot, Dad would fill a pan with water and have me cool my feet while I practiced. If I grew faint, he'd take a book and fan me, sometimes for three straight hours. When the weather turned bitter cold, he'd cover me with not only my coat but his as well. If my fingers were numb, he'd rub them until the circulation returned.

Most important, my father became my secret agent. He'd put on his police coat from Shenyang and con his way inside the conservatory, where parents were not allowed. There, he'd check the schedule to see who was giving a master class so he could sneak into it. If a security guard caught him and escorted him out, he'd linger in the hallway and quietly reenter the room when the guard was gone. If he was ejected a second time, he'd stand outside the classroom, pressing his ear against the doorway to hear what was being played and said. He'd do the same when a well-regarded teacher gave a private lesson.

In the evenings, he'd report his findings to me, and they were always helpful. For example, if he was able to observe a master class where an instructor was demonstrating a more lyrical way to phrase Chopin, he could explain that approach to me and patiently sit there while I put the lesson into practice.

"It isn't enough that we learn from Professor Zhao," he said. "Professor Zhao is just one of many teachers. He has a good approach, but if we learn the other approaches as well, and if we apply them to your technique, you'll be Number One."

My cousin Yifeng would listen to these discussions with amusement.

"You guys are so serious, Lang Lang," he'd say to me. "It's like the whole world depends on your being Number One."

"It does," I said.

"And if you're not?" he asked.

"I have to be. I will be."

And with that, I'd go off and practice.

■

I was finally feeling good again, but even in my happiest moments I would be vulnerable to an inconsolable sadness. Chinese New Year approached, a holiday when even the factory workers get to go home, and I wanted to spend it with my mother and grandparents, eating dumplings and watching the Chinese New Year spring show on TV with my cousins, a New Year's ritual. I hadn't seen my mother in six months.

"Can't we go home for just a day or two?" I asked my dad.

"No, all that time on the train will mean missing practice."

"Can't Mom come here?"

"No."

"Why not? I know she wants to see me."

"Because she has to work."

"Can't she get off?"

"No."

"Even for one day?"

"If she came here, she'd hurt your chances of getting into the conservatory," my father insisted. "She'd distract you. She'd coddle you. She'd make you weak with sentiment. Now you're getting strong and you need to get stronger. A doting mother would only soften your resolve."

In the fruit and vegetable market, I cried to Uncle No. 2. I begged him to get my father to change his mind. He was going home to his family for the holiday, and I thought he would sympathize. But Han simply told me what I already knew: that my father was a stubborn man. Han told me about an American movie called *Rocky*, where a prizefighter in training has to win a big match. Every day he thinks of nothing but running, exercising, punching the bag, and sparring. He can't be distracted by anything. Uncle No. 2 compared me to Rocky, and my dad to his trainer, whose job was to keep everyone away from him.

"Even my mom?" I asked him.

"Even your mom."

I knew Han was right. But that didn't ease the pain. Nothing would until I saw my mom again.

Red Paper
on a Bulletin Board

We were a week away from exams, and I'd never been more nervous in my life. Roughly three thousand students would be denied admittance to the fifth grade, and only twelve would be accepted. Kids from every part of China were auditioning, including the local stars from Beijing—some who had been playing for as long as I had been, some with reputations greater than mine, with more contest victories and far more confidence, some students with families who had lots of money and connections.

My practicing reached a fever pitch. When I was too nervous to fall asleep, I'd practice instead, sometimes until midnight. During one of those late-night sessions, I remembered a story Professor Angry had told me, and it disturbed me so deeply that I woke up my father.

"Professor Angry was judging an audition," I told Dad, "where a student was playing Bach's *Well-Tempered*

IN FRONT OF THE CENTRAL
CONSERVATORY OF MUSIC (IN
BEIJING)

Clavier. In the middle of the audition the telephone rang. The director of the school was trying to reach one of the judges, so the student was told to stop playing. When the judge hung up the phone, the student was instructed to start playing from the exact half beat where she'd been interrupted." I told my father that I was afraid this might be a trick the judges would pull to see just how good we were. I was afraid it would happen to me.

My father agreed with me. He suggested that we try it out—he would stop me at various points, I would wait for five minutes, and then pick up again without missing a beat. That way we would be prepared.

The stop-and-start training became part of my routine. When I mastered that technique, I regained my confidence, and all seemed to be going well. But then I remembered that Professor Angry would be one of the judges.

"She'll never admit me! She doesn't think I have talent!"

"She's not the only judge," Dad said. "There are others who are not prejudiced. They will overrule her. Besides, she hasn't heard you play in a year. You've improved dramatically. You'll win her over."

I didn't see how that would be possible. But something else was worrying me. We had never told Professor Zhao that I had studied with Professor Angry. When he had helped me with the admissions application, I had just mentioned Professor Zhu, not Professor Angry, when asked to list previous teachers. I was thinking of when my father had applied to the conservatory and had listed his wrong age and was denied admission.

My father tried to brush my worries aside, telling me not to confuse his life with mine. He assured me I would do fine at the audition and go on to enjoy a long and brilliant career. But that night I couldn't sleep. The next day would be the most important day of my life; everything we had been working toward, everything my family had sacrificed, was hanging on it. My mind was racing, imagining the devastation and humiliation I would feel—and that my father would never survive.

"Come to my bed," said my dad. "Sleep by my side."

I crawled in next to him. "Will you put your arm around me?" This was the first time in my life that I had asked my dad for affection. In my father's embrace, I was able to turn off the noise in my head, close my eyes, and find a place of quiet. That night I slept like a baby.

I awoke with the sun. I wanted to leave very early so we could get to the conservatory before anyone else, and Dad agreed.

Riding on the backseat of the bike, watching the endless city pass before me, the cars, trucks, buses, and motorcycles, old people and young people, policemen, workmen, professionals in suits, and peddlers in rags, I heard only the music I was about to play: Bach, Chopin's "Black-Key" études, a piece by the Russian composer Glinka called "The Nightingale." Over the music, I conjured up the image of Monkey King. Monkey King, my friend, my hero, was coming with me to the audition, Monkey King who could conquer any problem and win any contest. He would sit on the piano bench next to me as I played. Monkey King couldn't be defeated, and neither could I.

When we arrived at the conservatory, hundreds of kids and their parents were already lined up. As I looked them over, all I saw were the prodigies: *That boy over there looks like a genius. That girl standing behind him must also be a genius. Everyone has been practicing harder and longer than I have. The teachers will discover that I lied on the application. I'll be kicked out even before I play. Professor Angry will eliminate me the minute she sees me. She'll scream, "Lang Lang isn't talented! I told him last year and he didn't believe me! Send that kid back to Shenyang!"*

I started shaking as we got to the back of the line. My father grabbed my hand, squeezed it, and whispered, "You can shake all you want to now, but when your hands touch the piano, you must stop shaking and do what we came here to do. Do you understand?"

I nodded my head. I was too nervous to speak.

The line moved at a snail's pace. We stood there for two or three hours before I was able to get out a few words to my father. "There are so many kids applying," I said. "Everyone in China is applying."

"To be among the first group of applicants is easy," he explained. "You just send in a cassette tape. If it sounds decent to the judges, they let you come here to play. Of these thousands, all but forty will be eliminated."

We finally reached the building entrance, and once we were inside, we commenced another interminable wait to enter the room located next to the basketball court. Inch by inch, we stepped closer and closer to that room. Soon, I could hear students performing. Some sounded good. Some didn't. I tried not to listen to them, only to the music I had prepared, the music in my mind that would decide my future.

When the kids who had already auditioned emerged from the room, they stopped to speak to those of us still waiting. One girl said, "I did terribly. Everyone's doing terribly. The judges look at you with daggers in their eyes."

When she said that, I remembered my second competition, in Taiyuan, the one I didn't win. Some of the kids who had played before me then had spoken similarly: "I played poorly . . . Everyone is messing up . . . It's awful in there." They had been trying to spook me, and this girl was no different. In essence, she was saying, "I didn't perform well and neither will you."

When I finally entered the room, the first person I saw seated among the judges was Professor Angry. I couldn't look her in the eye, but I felt her glaring at me and I was scared. After my dad gave me his customary pat on the back, I walked straight to the grand piano, took a little bow before the judges, and sat. I envisioned Monkey King beside me, and I played.

Afterward, I wasn't so sure how I'd performed. My father and Uncle No. 2 kept reassuring me. "You will be in the top forty," they said. "There is no doubt." But I had doubts. What if Professor Angry had turned the other judges against me? What if they discovered I hadn't listed her on my application?

Two days passed before the conservatory posted the names of those who made the cut. The tradition is to tack a piece of red paper on a bulletin board with a list of the names of the forty students slated for round two in bold black ink.

"Lang Lang" was listed.

Seeing my name on that sheet of red, the Chinese color of good fortune, was an immense relief. Professor Angry had not done me in. I had passed one test, but the next was far tougher. Out of forty applicants, only twelve would be admitted. But being in the top twelve would not be enough, because only the top seven were given scholarships. Without one, I couldn't afford to attend the conservatory. Placing 8th would be no better than placing 2,500th.

What's more, the next level required more than playing. There were also written exams covering theory and harmony. A teacher would play a chord, and with your back turned, you'd have to name it: a third chord, a seventh chord, a dissonant chord, an augmented chord. Then there was the ordeal of repeating a rhythm pattern: a judge would quickly demonstrate, and you had to duplicate. That was not my strength. So I had much to worry about, and I had several days to do the worrying.

The final forty students were given practice rooms in the conservatory where we could rehearse our pieces. Because parents weren't allowed on campus, mothers and fathers, and sometimes grandparents, would stand outside the gates and yell encouragement, chastisements, and advice to their kids through the practice-room windows, like screaming fans at a sports event. Because of the one-child policy, every family was invested in the fate of its one child. "You're playing too fast! You're playing too slow! You're playing sloppily!" Some students, indifferent to the whole affair, would play with their right hand only and, with their left hand, play cards with a friend. Some parents who were not musical would scream instructions to a room, mistaking someone else's playing for their own kid's. Not my dad. My father never once confused me with anyone else. He knew my touch, my style, my phrasing. He knew more about my approach than I did, and when he yelled up instructions—"Play that last movement again, Lang Lang, only this time make it more legato"—I paid attention.

During those days before the second-round auditions, I was assigned a practice room far from the gates, which was bad because my father couldn't hear me and couldn't scream instructions.

"Try to exchange rooms with a student who's closer to the gates," my dad suggested after the first day. "I need to hear you practice."

The next day I walked down the hallway and asked several kids to trade rooms with me, but they wouldn't hear of it. Of course they wanted what I wanted—to let their parents critique them—and competition was fierce. I was about to give up and almost decided not to knock on the door of the room closest to the gate. What was the point? I was tired of getting dirty looks from the other kids. But I knocked anyway, and when the door opened, I recognized the boy facing me. He came from Shenyang and had placed second when I won the local contest at age five. He was older than I was and was already a student at the conservatory.

"Lang Lang," he said, "of course you can have this room. You *should* be closer to your dad. He can help you."

His gesture meant a great deal to me. Even in the cutthroat conservatory, some people were capable of being kind, and given all the jealousy and backbiting my dad and I had encountered from our Shenyang "friends," this act of kindness was all the more meaningful.

My father knew that the centerpiece of my second-round audition, a Mozart sonata, required extraordinary sensitivity, and by shouting out instructions, he helped me achieve that sensitivity. It sounds funny, and even contradictory, but somehow it worked.

My confidence was restored, but I still felt nervous. After all, this was it—do or die. On the eve of my callback, I returned to my father's bed to ask him to sleep with his arm around me, but even in his comforting embrace I slept fitfully, taunted by the fear that I would lose my chance, just as he had so many years before.

At daybreak we were awake, and by noon we were at the conservatory. By one I was taking the theory exams, and by three, after my father patted me on the back, I had bowed before the judges (including Professor Angry) and begun to play. For thirty minutes, I played as well as I had ever played in my life.

That night I dreamed of dragons chasing me. I ran through fire and flew through the sky. I skipped over dark clouds and threw lightning bolts back at the beasts. Then real thunder woke me up. A violent summer storm had hit Beijing, and we got soaked riding my dad's bike to the conservatory. Uncle No. 2 met us at the school; he wanted to be there when they posted the results.

With Han and my dad by my side, I walked into the main building. At the end of the main hall I could see that piece of red paper, and I could also hear kids and their parents crying. Some screamed curses. I suddenly couldn't go on. I couldn't bear to see if my name was among the top twelve, let alone the top seven. Dad and Uncle No. 2 walked ahead of me, breaking into a trot and then a full-out sprint. I watched them scan the list from bottom to top.

Silence.

Then a shout.

"Lang Lang!" screamed Uncle No. 2 joyously. "You're number one!"

For the first time since we had moved to Beijing, some eighteen months earlier, I saw my father smile.

I started jumping up and down and ran to see my name at the top of that red piece of paper. When I saw it, I screamed the loudest scream of my life. I wanted to hug somebody. When I did, it was Uncle No. 2, not Dad. Then we telegrammed my mother the news.

Beginning Again

"The competition is just getting started," my father told me.

"What do you mean?" I asked him. "I already made number one."

"Yes, that was for your school ranking. That was good."

"Better than good," I said, correcting him. "It's great. We don't have to pay tuition, and my lessons with Professor Zhao are now free."

"Lang Lang, one victory is not enough. Besides, you didn't win a contest. You just won admission to the conservatory."

"But it was everything we were working for." What more could he want?

"There's something bigger," my father said. "There's a contest being held in Beijing. It's the Xing Hai national piano competition, and we have to start getting ready now."

My father had promised that we could spend forty days in Shenyang after the admissions exams. I hadn't been home in over a year and a half. Now he told me we would go for only twenty days. He believed Shenyang had too many distractions, even though we had already agreed that I would practice four hours in the morning and four hours in the afternoon each day we would be there. I was allowed two hours a day for visiting my grandparents, other relatives, and friends.

Though I was disappointed, I was still eager to go home. My father had kept my mother away for the three months preceding the entrance exams, and whatever price I would have to pay to feel her arms around me was worth it. I was dying to see her.

On the Friday morning of our departure, the sky opened up and rain flooded the entire city. We were due in Shenyang that night, but all the trains were either delayed or canceled. We didn't pull in to Shenyang until Sunday. My mother hadn't heard from us, so she was frightened, imagining we had vanished in the floods. When we finally arrived home, she cried for joy.

But her joy didn't last. I came down with a dangerously high fever, so high that I was rushed to the hospital. In my delirium, I was afraid I'd never get well, never be able to play the piano again or see my friends.

"Of course you will," said my father, standing by the side of my bed, and for a moment it seemed he cared only about my well-being, only that his son would be healthy. But then he continued. "No fever can stop you. Nothing can stop you. You'll get well and practice, and you'll be number one in the Xing Hai national piano competition."

In those feverish days, I had many dreams. In some, Bach spoke to me. He spoke in Chinese, urging me on, encouraging me to fight through my sickness so I could go back to practicing. He spoke with great authority, and I believed him, but I was mostly just thrilled that Bach knew my name.

When I finally left the hospital, Miss Feng, my beloved teacher, had a party for me in her classroom and invited all my old friends. They came to congratulate me on my admission to the conservatory, and though I enjoyed their good wishes, I couldn't stop thinking about this new contest and the amount of work that would be required to win. The same was true when I visited my grandparents. I loved seeing them and I loved the way they doted on me, yet I was preoccupied with getting home and practicing. I had lost almost a week in the hospital and was behind the practice schedule that my father had established.

When my dad first mentioned the competition, I had had reservations. Now, though, I had none. Since I had taken first place in the auditions, I wanted to repeat that feat. I liked the taste of victory; I relished the idea of vanquishing all my competitors.

During my brief time home, I had a few lessons with Professor Zhu, who helped me prepare the material I would play for the Xing Hai contest. As always, she lifted my spirits while calming me down.

"Lang Lang," she said, "you must keep a good balance between being a gifted pianist and being a happy young boy. You must not forget to play with your friends, enjoy your toys, and read the stories that excite your imagination."

"There is no time for anything but practicing, Professor Zhu," I said.

"Is that you talking," she asked, "or your father? After this concert there will be another contest, and then another."

"And I have to be number one in all of them."

"Well, maybe you will and maybe you won't. Contests aren't always fair, and talent doesn't always win out." What mattered most, she told me, was bringing the beauty of music to others. Contests were merely stepping-stones. My talent wouldn't disappear no matter where I placed in any competition.

At some level, I knew that Professor Zhu was right. But my father had told me that if I didn't place first in the Xing Hai contest, he wouldn't allow my mother to visit me in Beijing for an entire year, and I had no doubt that he would stick to his word. I had to keep practicing. I had to win; I had to have my mother near. And besides, I wanted to be Number One.

■

After twenty happy days at home, I returned to Beijing, my full strength restored, and began to prepare in earnest. Because I was officially a scholarship winner and a student in the conservatory, I got to play for many piano teachers, each of whom critiqued me. Once again my father donned his police uniform and worked his way into the halls of the school. When he heard the other students being critiqued, he took careful notes. He also observed new teaching techniques and imparted them to me in precise detail. Even though I was now an official conservatory student, my father placed his trust in no one but himself.

He made friends with the youngest member of the teaching staff, Mr. Zhang. The Beijing conservatory was extremely conservative; the older professors had been there a very long time and weren't likely to give extra attention to a young kid without money or connections. My placing first in the auditions made no difference—in fact, it inspired resentment. But Mr. Zhang was young and not part of the established hierarchy; he related to me and my dad. He was open-minded, with a great love of music and an extensive CD collection. He was also among the most intelligent listeners of music I have ever encountered. He'd hear nuances that even my talented father and I would miss. Above all that, Mr. Zhang believed in me, and along with Uncle No. 2 he became an official member of the small but devoted Lang Lang team. With that growing support system I felt invincible, and the Xing Hai competition felt less and less like a competition at all.

One day, though, I learned that a student named Yang, who was a grade higher than I, was entering the competition and, worse, was playing the same piece as I was—the Czerny étude op. 740, no. 31. Yang was the boy who, when I was seven, had walked away with the grand-prize piano as I walked away with that yellow toy dog. He had beaten me once. Could I beat him now?

"Never!" the kids in my class taunted me. "He's better than you. He's number one in the sixth grade, and the best in the sixth grade always beats the best in the fifth grade. You don't stand a chance!"

"Don't listen to the kids," my father said. "They want to plant doubt in your head so you'll make mistakes. Just keep practicing."

But how could I not worry when I was dealt another blow? Of the twenty students competing, I was slated to play second. It's far better to perform toward the end of a contest rather than at the beginning so you can hear your competitors before you perform.

"I'm not sure I can do it," I told my dad. "The students who come after me will hear how I've played and figure out how to play better. I won't be able to sleep tonight. I'm too worried."

"You will sleep with my arm around you. You will sleep well. When you wake, you'll be rested, and before you walk onstage, I will pat you on your back, the way I always do. You will play flawlessly, brilliantly. You will win."

Eight hundred people came to view the competition. It was held in an auditorium on the campus of the conservatory. The judges were almost the same group that had judged the entry auditions, Professor Angry among them. She hadn't been able to keep me from placing first the last time I stood before her; maybe this time she would thwart me.

I played the Czerny, a Chopin waltz, a Bach prelude and fugue, a Beethoven sonata, and a Chinese piece. I thought I played well, but by then I had lost all objectivity. When I was through, I could hear the applause from my dad, Han, Mr. Zhang, and my cousin, but in that large auditorium their applause sounded weak compared with the thunderous applause for the other students, who had brought armies of family and friends. Yang played exceptionally well, and though it was hard to compare his skills with mine, I couldn't forget how he had beaten me once before.

I had to wait until the next day to learn the results. There would be six winners: three third places, two second places, and one first place. Whoever took first place would receive a black-and-white television. I desperately wanted one, to watch cartoons and soccer.

When we arrived at the conservatory the next day, the results were not ready, we were told, because of arguments among the judges. My mind spun out of control. What were the judges debating? Was Professor Angry campaigning against me? We waited for a torturous hour, then two, then three, then four. It got so late that I couldn't keep my eyes open, so Uncle No. 2 took me home. Dad and Mr. Zhang stayed.

I don't know what time it was when I was awakened, but I do remember that I didn't know whether or not I was still dreaming because my father was above me, smiling.

"Number One," he said.

"Am I dreaming?" I had to ask.

"You are awake, and you have won."

Mr. Zhang was standing next to my dad. "When the judges finally came out of the room," said Mr. Zhang, "the woman you call Professor Angry was the first to see us. I asked her, 'Who won?' 'Lang Lang,' she said. 'Did you vote for him?' I asked. 'Yes,' she said, 'I had to. I could no longer deny his talent.'"

The Kung Fu Master of Eight Regions

We had now moved to an even worse neighborhood in Beijing, to be close to the conservatory. The walls of the one room in which my father, my cousin, and I lived were even thinner than before, and mice ran freely through them. The room never saw sunlight, and we shared a toilet, which was always broken, with five other families. The smell when you entered the building was truly disgusting. It was no surprise that the neighbors were not music lovers.

Still, I was excited to have a TV again and thrilled to watch Brazil beat Italy on penalty kicks in the final game of the World Cup. My father even let me watch cartoons every evening from 6:30 to 7:00. But the best result of my winning the Xing Hai competition was that my father allowed my mother to visit us in Beijing. She must have despaired when she saw our new living quarters, but she never complained. The first thing she did was take me to the toy store for a new Transformer.

And yet despite her pride in me—having won the competition, I was now considered the best pianist in

MONKEY KING'S KUNG FU MOVE

China between the ages of nine and twelve—and despite the joy I felt because of her visit, I couldn't relax. My father kept track of every contest, and he had recently learned of an international competition that was coming up soon. "The national is nothing," my father said to me, "the international is everything." Though I begged my mother to come live with us, she told me it wasn't so easy to find work in Beijing. She promised to visit every two or three months. We would continue to write letters to each other. "Your father only wants what's best for you," she told me. "Most dads don't care half as much as he does."

I knew she was right. Dad was relentless, difficult, cold. But he was also my best ally, my strength. When I walked into a room to compete and felt his pat on my back, I felt braver. With my father on my side, I knew I had a real chance at being Number One.

The China International Piano Competition was an entirely new experience. Anyone under eighteen could compete, and I wasn't even eleven. My dad had identified my three chief rivals, all of whom studied at the conservatory: two boys, Zhai and Ming, and a girl named Hong. They were already playing famously difficult pieces by Liszt and Rachmaninoff. They were deep into Beethoven's late sonatas, and I was just beginning the early ones. I didn't see how I could beat them.

"By practicing harder," said my dad.

"There are only so many hours in a day!" I said.

"More concentration means more progress," he argued. "You must treat each hour of practice as a precious commodity. Not a minute must be wasted."

I was a confident child, but I was also realistic. Zhai and Ming had already won international contests, and Zhai had placed first at the Stravinsky Competition in the United States. I'd heard them play many times at the conservatory, and they were extraordinary. We were all eager to represent our conservatory in the next level of the competition, but to do so, we would have to place in the top four. It wouldn't be easy.

I needed extra help, and I found it in audiobooks by a mysterious kung fu master, Tung Lin, who reminded me of Monkey King except that he was human. Each region of China has its own master, but Tung Lin calls himself Master of Eight Regions because he has taken techniques from each master and incorporated them into his own unbeatable style. He reigns over everyone. I thought of Tung Lin's approach when I practiced. In my mind, I called Zhai, with his incredible technique and four years of seniority, Master of the North Region. I called Ming Master of the South Region. I learned from my rivals the same way Tung Lin learned from his. I took the best of what they did and transformed it to make it mine. I declared myself their superior: Piano Master of Eight Regions, the Pink-Faced King of Chinese Piano.

It was a game, but it made practicing easier. Each day I'd listen to another kung fu tale of how to become the master of masters, and as I slaved away, I dreamed I lived those adventures and experienced those battles. I knew that to beat the big kids required the heart of a warrior.

By then, of course, I knew the routine. The weeks before the contest were crazy: There was school. And then I would eat, sleep, and breathe piano. Never stop. Never think of anything except the notes dancing through my head. Fixate on flawless playing. Count the days, the hours, and the minutes before it was time to perform.

I depended on what had become our ritual: the night before, I slept with my father's arm around my shoulders; before I walked onstage to play, my father patted me on the back; and when I reached the piano, I invoked the image of a fellow soldier. Before it was Monkey King. Now it was Tung Lin.

At the competition, I played a Chopin rondo, and the reviews were ecstatic.

"Who is this little kid?"

"My God, I can't believe he's playing as well as kids five and six years older!"

"Where did he come from?"

"He's remarkable."

But in the end, I placed fifth. I would not represent the conservatory in the top four and go on to the next level. I was out. Zhai, Ming, and Hong were in, and so was another girl I thought I had bested. The judges said that because she was nearly eighteen, this would be her last chance. I'd have other chances, they said, but naturally I didn't see it that way. I thought talent was supposed to win, regardless of circumstance.

"You were definitely in the top four," my dad said, "but life isn't always fair. All we can do is move on. Professor Zhao knows about another international competition we can start preparing for right away. It's a more important contest than this one." His calm surprised me. It seemed that at some point he had stopped doubting my abilities, and now my failure was someone else's fault, not mine.

A month later, the students who had placed in the top four were eliminated in the next round of the China International Piano Competition, which meant that Beijing's Central Conservatory of Music would not be represented in the finals. I couldn't help but think that I, Piano Master of Eight Regions, could have made it to the finals, that the judges had made a mistake by eliminating me so early.

But my disappointment was overshadowed by my excitement about this next contest, which would be held in Germany. For the first time in my life, I would be entering the enchanted land of Beethoven, Bach, and Brahms.

BEYOND

CHINA

Germany

It was the summer of 1994, I was twelve, and I was sure I was dreaming. Germany was too strange, too exotic. I felt a million miles away from China, on a different planet where everything looked and smelled fresh and wonderful.

After I had lost the China International Piano Competition in Beijing, I had been heartbroken, but I was also encouraged when the judges praised me so highly. Uncle No. 2 further bolstered my spirits when he said, "Lang Lang, consider what you've done in the past year. You were number one in the entrance auditions for the conservatory. You were number one in the national competition. And you did well in this last contest against students much older than you. Six months ago no one knew who you were. Now everyone knows you."

What he'd said was true, but I still had a long way to go. I had not yet won an international competition, and that was my dad's next goal. When he told me about the Fourth International Competition for Young Pianists in Germany, he was so optimistic that any doubt I may have had was quelled.

Because I hadn't placed in the top four of the Beijing competition, I couldn't get a national sponsorship to pay for my travel. My father worked tirelessly to raise money for my trip. He spoke with my mom and many of our relatives, insisting that I would be number one in this contest, if only we could get to Germany. Being number one in a competition outside of China would, according to Dad, change everything. It would catapult me into a higher category and set me up for greater things.

It took several weeks, but my parents were able to raise the necessary five thousand dollars—three thousand from relatives and two thousand from a bank—which included the cost of Professor Zhao's travel expenses. My father decided that I'd have a better chance at winning if my teacher came along to continue training me while we were overseas. With so much riding on me, I couldn't afford to lose. The thought of Europe energized me, and I wanted to do nothing but practice.

The week before we took off, a famous female piano teacher gave us a farewell party in Beijing, which I saw as a huge vote of confidence. My main supporters—Dad, Uncle No. 2, Mr. Zhang, and Professor Zhao—were all there.

"I'm glad you're going to Germany," said the teacher. "And I'm sure you'll do well. Just don't expect to be number one."

Her words were knives through my heart.

"Why not?" I asked. In my mind I was now invincible.

"Lang Lang," she said, "hasn't anyone told you whom you'll be competing against?"

"No."

"Zhe and Yu."

Zhe and Yu were four years older than I was and far more accomplished than Zhai, Ming, and Hong, the pianists who had beaten me in the last contest. They were considered the best in China.

"The government is paying for Zhe and Yu to represent China in the contest," said the teacher. "They are proven winners."

That night, after the party, I couldn't sleep. "You didn't tell me that Zhe and Yu were going to Germany," I told my father.

"It's good that they're going," he said.

"How can you say that?"

"I say it, Lang Lang, because you'd have to face them sooner or later. And sooner is better than later. In Germany, the judges don't know who Zhe and Yu are, or who is sponsored by the nation, or who paid out of their own pocket. They have no expectations. They will judge on talent alone."

Their repertoires were staggering, including impossibly difficult pieces by Liszt and Weber, not to mention the piano version of Stravinsky's *Petrushka*. Professor Zhao had chosen challenging compositions for me by Chopin and Liszt, but they were far less dazzling than what my champion competitors would be performing.

"Mastering technical intricacies does not win competitions," my teacher said. "Total musicality is what wins."

Just don't expect to be Number One. I kept hearing the voice of the famous female teacher in my head. *Just don't expect to be Number One*, a mantra of fear, had to be replaced with *You must be Number One.* But how? Could Monkey King prevail in Germany? And what about the kung fu masters? Their realm was China, not Europe. Europe was the birthplace of the music that had informed every moment of my young life. That meant that not only would Zhe and Yu be superior to me but so would an army of students from Spain, France, Italy, Russia, the United States, and Germany itself, students who had been raised on the music of their own heritage.

"It's *your* native music as well," said my dad. "You were raised on it just as they were. You heard it when you were in your mother's womb. It's universal music; it belongs to anyone who loves it. Now stop thinking so negatively and go back to practicing."

Of course I practiced, only stopping when Dad and I went to the German embassy for visas. My father told me we had nothing to worry about; issuing visas was a routine matter.

"You have every reason to be concerned," said the German

embassy official looking over our papers. "You have no health insurance and no money in the bank, and without them we cannot issue visas for you and your son."

"Can't you overlook that?" asked my dad. "My son is competing in the Fourth International Competition for Young Pianists in Germany."

"But he's not representing China, right? If that were the case, I could overlook the insurance issue. Earlier, two other students came in for their visas with blue government passports. You have red passports. Why isn't your son representing China? Is he not good enough?"

"He's already won important competitions in China," my father answered, sidestepping the question.

"And another thing," said the man. "You have no job. We are not inclined to allow unemployed foreigners into Germany. Why don't you have a job?"

"My job is to make sure my son becomes the number one piano player in the world."

"That isn't a job. That's a wild dream."

"A dream that you'll destroy if you don't let us into Germany," my father insisted.

"Rules are rules."

"Rules can be bent."

"Not by me."

My father's eyes betrayed his fury. I could see that he was silently trying to figure out what to do, and I was glad he was there to overcome obstacles like this when they presented themselves, because I had worked myself up into a feverish state over this competition. My father had convinced me that I could beat those older boys, and I was dead set on proving it.

"I will figure out something," my father said to me as we left the embassy. "We will get those visas."

At that moment, a security guard stopped my father. "I couldn't help but overhear your conversation," he told him. "I think I recognize your accent. Are you from the north of China?"

"Yes, from Shenyang."

The guard told us he was from Dong Feng, a city north of Shenyang—my grandfather's hometown. When my father mentioned my grandfather's name, the guard recognized it. My great-grandfather had founded the middle school this man had attended.

My father and the security guard became instant buddies, chatting for a half hour about people they knew in common. Then my father got down to brass tacks. "Look," he said, "you heard our plight. My son here is nothing less than a genius. To keep him from entering this contest on a technicality would be a crime. Is there any way you can help us?"

The guard, who had worked at the embassy for many years, knew the lenient officials from the strict ones and offered to introduce us to a friendly one. The guard was sure this man would grant us visas when he heard our story.

The lenient officer listened to us and made an exception, but getting our visas was only the first of many hurdles. Standing directly in front of me in line at passport control—out of all the people at the Beijing international airport—were Zhe and Yu. They didn't turn around and look at me, but even if they had, I'm not sure they'd have known who I was.

When they showed their passports, the official responded with excitement. "Diplomatic passports!" he cried. "You must be representing China. In what capacity?"

They explained that they were piano players on their way to an international competition.

"Our country is proud of you," the man told them. "I'm certain you'll return home with high honors. Go right through and take my best wishes with you."

I was no Zhe or Yu—I was a short, pudgy twelve-year-old who could barely see over the passport counter.

"Why are you going to Germany?" asked the official.

"I'm going to that same piano competition."

"Why don't you have a diplomatic passport like the other two?"

"The government is paying for them. My family is paying for me."

"Does that mean you aren't as good as they are?"

"He will be Number One," Dad answered when my rising anger kept me from responding.

"That sounds like a father's wishful thinking," the official said as he issued us through.

It was my first time flying. Despite having grown up on the Air Force base, I had never been on a plane before. It was a dream come true. When I saw Zhe and Yu sitting in big comfortable seats up front, I presumed that the two empty seats across from them were for me and Dad. I went to sit down, but then a stewardess stopped me.

"Are you business-class?" she asked.

I didn't understand what she meant.

"No. We are economy," my father said as he steered me deeper into the plane.

We marched down the entire length of the huge aircraft until we reached the very last row, where the seats were tiny and, once the plane took off, the noise from the engines screamed into our ears. We flew through thunderstorms and turbulence; the plane shook, dropped, and lurched. I clutched my father's hand. I squeezed my eyes closed. I feared for my life. I envisioned the plane cracking in half; the first- and business-class passengers would parachute safely to the ground while the economy passengers would be sucked into the plane's giant jets and burned alive.

Once in Germany, my mood did not brighten. We stood at the back of a long customs line while Yu and Zhe were greeted by a welcoming committee. They were whisked right through, no questions asked. My father was glum, preoccupied with the debt he had incurred. He kept telling me I could beat Yu and Zhe, but I knew that he was fully aware of how good they were. Almost all our money had been spent on airfare, and we had little left for room and board. On our first night we stayed in a dormitory room on the outskirts of Frankfurt lent to us by a relative of one of Professor Zhao's students. My dad and I slept on the floor; Professor Zhao slept on the bed.

Jet lag hit me hard. I woke up at five in the morning, got dressed, and took a walk around the block before my father or my teacher got up. I couldn't wait to see this country of my dreams, no matter that I had no idea where we were and couldn't speak the language. As the sky turned from black to gray to blue, I felt as if I were in a movie. A blue sky was new to me. Fresh air was new to me. The signs in German, the Audis and Porsches and Volkswagens zipping around corners, the smell of fresh coffee and sugary strudel coming from the cafés, the blond-haired women walking to work—Europe had engaged every one of my senses in completely new ways, and I was dizzy with the experience.

We would make our way to Frankfurt proper, then take a train to Ettlingen, where the competition would be held. How different even the trains were in Germany—people spoke quietly, no pushing, no shoving, no loud arguments. I sat next to the window and watched the countryside hurry by: deep green forests, winding rivers, a distant castle on a hill. As the train whistled and sped through that exotic land of cities and villages, valleys and factories, I heard every piece by Beethoven that I knew. Beethoven was the soundtrack to my day; his exciting rhythms, the explosion of his lyrical sounds, the sweep of his imagination, and the beauty of his musical voice, big and grand and never afraid, were constantly in my head. As the train raced on, I felt my fear diminishing, disappearing into the German countryside. I had found a second home, a place that I understood and a place that understood me. The Great Adventure had begun.

We had no hotel reservations in Frankfurt. I don't know why my father and my teacher hadn't planned ahead; maybe they thought we could make a train connection to Ettlingen, our final destination, or maybe they hadn't fully thought the trip through due to their inexperience with international travel. But the last train for Ettlingen had already left. We had no idea where to go from the train station, two Chinese men and a Chinese kid wandering around Frankfurt. Yet I was ecstatic. We passed old beer gardens and ancient churches, the river Main, which ran through the city, dazzling skyscrapers, cobblestoned streets. I was overjoyed to be in the holy land of classical music, and I ran ahead of my father and my teacher, who seemed tense and uncertain.

Just when it must have seemed to my father that we were completely lost, our mysterious good fortune once again prevailed. Who knows why I decided to take a left turn down that particular street in Frankfurt? I can't say. But there, at the end of the block, stood a man who looked Chinese washing a big sedan. I couldn't have been more surprised, and I gave him a friendly greeting. I asked him—in Mandarin—whether in fact he was Chinese.

"I am!" said the man proudly. "And so are you! What brings you to Frankfurt?"

I told him that we were passing through on our way to Ettlingen, where I was playing in the international piano contest.

"Piano!" exclaimed the man. "I love the piano! My daughter is learning piano. You must come to my house and play. You must be very good to have traveled all the way from China."

"Really? Can we really come to your house?"

"Of course. Who are your companions?" he asked, pointing to my father and Professor Zhao, who were hurrying down the street to catch up to me.

"My dad and my teacher."

"You're all welcome," he said, offering his hand. "I am Huang."

By then my father and Professor Zhao had caught up with me. They were surprised and delighted when Huang repeated his invitation. After a few cordial words, we packed our suitcases in the trunk, climbed into his car, and sped off to the suburbs of Frankfurt.

I didn't know about the suburbs until I saw them for myself. I didn't understand that a family could have a large freestanding house with a yard and garden just outside the city. It was a thrilling discovery.

Huang's house was huge. As the proprietor of three restaurants in Frankfurt, he had prospered. His home was filled with lovely Chinese furniture, red silk drapes, and blue velvet sofas. Best of all, though, was the first thing we saw when we walked through the door: a statue of Guan Yu, my father's hero, the most faithful and dedicated warrior general of the Shu Kingdom during the Three Kingdoms period of ancient China.

"Guan Yu!" exclaimed my dad. "He's my inspiration!"

"Mine as well," said Huang. "He's the symbol of victory and faithfulness."

"Victory at all costs," my father agreed.

"Lang Guoren, we are of one mind. You, your son, and Professor Zhao must stay in my house, as my guests, so Lang Lang can properly prepare to do battle in Ettlingen."

We accepted the invitation gratefully, and I agreed to give his daughter, who was nine, a piano lesson each day we stayed. I also gave little concerts for Huang and his family. Even though they knew I had traveled far for the competition and was a serious pianist, they were surprised by my talent. We were thrilled to have discovered each other.

The food Huang served was scrumptious. What could be better? A big house in the woody suburbs, a beautiful guest bedroom and private bath, a superb piano I was able to practice on six hours a day, people from home. And I even got to play Game Boy with Huang's little nephew. I wanted to stay forever.

After a week's stay, it was time to head to Ettlingen. Ever the perfect host, Huang insisted that he drive us there in his sedan.

"The train will be uncomfortable," he said. "And besides, you should travel in style like the winner that you are."

Before I got into his car, I noticed his license plates—8888. Four eights mean good fortune in Chinese culture. Everything about Huang was encouraging. He symbolized the positive side of chance. By chance, I had bumped into him. By chance, he loved the piano. "But it is fate, Lang Lang," he insisted, "that has allowed me to come to your aid."

In the woods outside Ettlingen, we were hosted—or, as the organizers of the contest called it, given a "homestay"—by an older couple who lived with a German shepherd that loved listening to Beethoven. During breakfast we'd eat delicious sausages while Beethoven's Sixth Symphony serenaded us from the stereo. I'd walk outside and wander around the woods, talking to the ghosts of the masters who had changed my life, rearranged my fate, and brought me here. The smell of freshly cut grass and blooming wildflowers, the great trees of the German forest, the puffy white clouds floating overhead—I'd never felt so happy and free.

Then another miracle:

Sponsors of the contest provided the contestants with rehearsal space. When we arrived at the building in Ettlingen that housed the practice rooms, we were met by the sound of music, which, like so many hummingbirds, fluttered out into the summer air. My father and I walked down the hall to find the room I was assigned, but suddenly my father stopped outside the half-open door of an occupied chamber.

"Listen to this playing," he said, amazed. "It's magical."

My father was right. When we looked in, I saw a Japanese pianist, perhaps eighteen years old, swaying back and forth in a kind of free-form dance as he played. I realized he was blind.

Intrigued, I sat down on the bench next to the young man. He turned his head toward me, his eyes squinted closed. In broken English, he asked me where I came from. My English was no better than his, but I managed to tell him that I was Chinese. Given the history of our two countries, I wondered if that fact would put him off, but he simply smiled and said, "Play."

I hesitated, but my dad whispered to me, "This is a great chance. He will show you things. Play for him."

I played from Liszt's "Tarantella," the story of a poisonous spider. In order to survive its bite, you must do a dance that shakes off the deadly poison, and thus you move in ways you've never moved before. The young man smiled as I played and swayed to the music. When I was through, he said, "Yes, yes, very good, very good."

Then he played the same piece, except it was entirely different. His touch was softer, more delicate, far more sensitive to the keys. He wasn't trying to capture the emotions; he *became* the emotions. The joy of playing came from his heart, not his head or even his fingers. He embodied the colorful melodies, the frenetic rhythms, the desperate story, the wild movements.

"Please play more," he said to me.

I played the Neapolitan song of the "Tarantella," trying to mimic the sensitivity he had shown.

"I don't know this part," he said.

But as I continued to play, he put his hands on the keys and began accompanying me. He created harmonies—right there on the spot—that augmented the song, infusing it with deeper beauty.

By this point in my life I had heard hundreds of pianists, but I had never heard anyone play like him. And his personality was as beautiful as his playing, easy and welcoming. When I told him my age, he said, "I'm lucky you are in the younger group or else you would beat me."

"I'm the lucky one," I said. "You're unbeatable."

For the next hour, we played for each other. The exchange didn't have the feeling of a contest; we were sharing our mutual love of music. Witnessing his sightless touch was one of the great lessons of my life: there were more ways to see the world than I had known.

I kept this in mind during a series of private lessons from Professor Zhao. The lessons were good, but my mind circled back to that Japanese youth and the inspiration he had given me. Then, the day before I was to play in the great Baroque concert hall, I performed the "Tarantella" for my teacher.

"My God, Lang Lang!" he said. "There's a wrong note in there. You've learned the piece with a wrong note!"

I wasn't upset, because I was feeling the piece as I had never felt it before. Thanks to my Japanese friend, I had discovered the soul of the composition. Besides, when one practices as many hours as I had, it's difficult to unlearn something. To take out that wrong note might have upset the whole construction of the piece for me. It might do more damage than good.

"You must relearn it!" Professor Zhao insisted.

I explained my reservations. He thought about what I said. "You may be right, Lang Lang. Go with your instincts. Your emotions are very heightened right now, and I don't want to upset you."

That night my German hostess, a religious woman, asked whether I would accompany her to church. I was raised in the Buddhist tradition, though my family was not religious, and had never been in a church before. I was curious and touched by her request, so I agreed. The church, a simple building with stained-glass windows, was situated in the Black Forest among tall trees and running brooks. Inside, I heard strains of Bach played on the organ, and it made perfect sense. In my mind, Bach and God were best friends. The church was empty except for an older woman who silently prayed as she knelt before a large crucifix.

This was my first encounter with a sculpted image of the crucified Christ. In the barracks when I was a small boy, the mother of one of my friends was a Christian who often told me the story of Jesus, but it didn't quite make sense to me—God sacrificing his own son. Standing before the crucifix, I thought of the powerful relationship between the Western music I loved so much and this tortured god. I knew that love for Jesus was deeply ingrained in many of the compositions I held dear, and I wanted to understand why and how. In truth, I couldn't. "This is the god," my hostess whispered to me, "who died because he loved all mankind."

"Can I pray to him?" I asked. I felt there was a deep spirit in this serene church in the woods.

"Of course. He answers all prayers."

She taught me how to make the sign of the cross, which I did before praying that in tomorrow's contest I would place first.

The concert hall the next morning, with its ornate Baroque architecture, was grander than any concert hall I'd ever seen. I imagined Brahms conducting his own symphonies onstage. I was slated to play before Yu and Zhe, which put me at a disadvantage, but there was nothing I could do about it. When my dad patted me on the back, as always, his pat gave me courage; this time, though, it also reminded me of the inspiration I had drawn from my Japanese friend. The sweetness of his musical soul had changed my approach, had made me more sensitive, and had given me something I'd never had before—a sense of poetry.

That afternoon in Ettlingen, Germany, I played first the Haydn Sonata in C Major, then a Chinese piece called the "Liu Yang River," a Chopin waltz, and finally the Liszt "Tarantella." The pianist isn't always the best judge of his own performance, but I knew I had played well. I had certainly played lyrically. I had at my command a lightness that surprised even me. I danced through the pieces, especially the Liszt, with tremendous confidence, and when I was through, the concert hall erupted in applause. I had never been received like that before—I was called back to take five separate bows. They wouldn't let me leave, and I wondered if they were demanding an encore. I began to walk back onto the stage, but one of the stagehands pulled me back, and the audience and judges erupted in laughter. I didn't know that in competitions encores are strictly forbidden.

Yu's and Zhe's performances were tremendous, absolutely brilliant. I was afraid that their technical skills made me look weak in comparison, but at the same time, though I was only twelve, I felt secure. I felt that my Japanese friend, who was the last in a string of blessings handed to me on a trip that had endured on such good fortune, had given me a gift that all the skill in the world could not top. I appreciated the ferocity with which Yu and Zhe played, their killer concentration, their absolute mastery of the compositions. But I also felt them trying too hard. Their effort was compromising their interpretations. Their interpretations, at least to my ears, lacked heart.

I was sitting next to Professor Zhao in the first rows and my father was sitting in the balcony when it was time to announce the winners. A gentleman made his way to the microphone and spoke in German, so I couldn't understand his remarks, but I knew that the tradition was to give five prizes. Sometimes, if the judges didn't feel any contestant had met the highest criteria, they would not award a first prize. That had happened several times in recent years.

They began with the consolation prizes, which were awarded to a Ukrainian, a Lithuanian, and a Spaniard.

Then the big prizes.

The first was for fifth place—which went to one of the Chinese boys, Zhe. He started crying.

Fourth place was next—the name of a Russian boy was announced.

Then third—a French girl.

Second place was big. It meant defeat. I put my hands over my ears when they announced it, terrified of hearing my name.

My teacher nevertheless whispered into my ear a translation of what our German host was saying. "Second place is from China," he said.

Oh, no! I thought. *Not second place!*

"Second place goes to Yu," Professor Zhao said.

I was as relieved as Yu was furious, but at the same time I couldn't be certain I would be number one. There was a long silence.

As we waited, I thought of the man at the German embassy; I thought of the customs official; I thought of the way Zhe and Yu must have smiled to themselves when I tried to sit across from them in business class. If I didn't take first place, or if there was no first-place winner, I would be devastated. Not only that, I didn't know what would become of us. We would be in irreparable debt.

But the German broke his silence. I leaned over to my professor for his translation. "It's been a very good competition this year, and we are pleased with the quality of our contestants. It was very difficult deciding who would win. As you know, some years we have forgone awarding first place because we didn't want to discredit the quality of our top prize. To be number one requires a truly extraordinary performance. We are pleased to announce that we do have a number one winner."

My heart thumped so loudly I was certain everyone could hear it.

"This year," the host continued, "one player towered above all the others, although he is a short little guy. This year we are proud to give the number one prize and five thousand German marks to . . ."

Another pause, another moment of excruciating suspense.

"Lang . . . Lang." Amid the German, I heard my name clearly.

I jumped up and hugged my teacher, but he shushed me so that he could keep interpreting as the host continued his speech.

"But there is more," the man said. "This year we are also award-ing Lang Lang a special prize for the most outstanding artistic perfor-mance in the history of our competition, including four thousand German marks."

Two prizes! And one created just for me! I was dizzy with the thought that I had triumphed over the highest-ranked pianists in China, Yu and Zhe. I began jumping up and down, screaming.

A famous Chinese piano professor I recognized came up to me. He had trained his own students to win this contest, and he must have been disappointed, but with great sincerity and kindness he said, "Lang Lang, I've never heard anyone play as you played. God was moving your fingers. God was whispering in your ear."

Someone sitting in the balcony next to Dad had a video camera and filmed my father's reaction. I didn't see the video until years later, and when I did, I was shocked: he was weeping, racked with sobs, his face covered with tears. I never saw him like that before or ever again. But on the afternoon my victory was announced, it wasn't my father I sought out—it was my Japanese friend, the pianist with the beautiful touch. I found him seated in the back of the auditorium. I hugged him and said, "Thank you. I'll never forget you."

And I never have.

Chopin

A twelve-year-old boy has an ego. So does a fifty-year-old teacher. And they are fragile things. In three short years, I went from being fired by one teacher to winning two major competitions. If my ego had once been deflated, now it threatened to burst. How could it be otherwise?

My father's ego, of course, swelled with mine. He had always loved to boast about my achievements, especially to the parents of my colleagues, but now that he had more to brag about—and perhaps because he did so in a booming voice—he became an unpopular figure among the families of my classmates. At the same time, they wanted him to listen to and evaluate their own children. He became a kind of unofficial professor at the school.

The teachers were a proud bunch, too. Their reputations were tied to their students; the more winners they had, the more exalted their status. Professor Zhao's status at the conservatory rose considerably when I placed first in Germany. Like my dad, he bragged about his contribution to my development, and that was perfectly understandable.

It was also understandable that I would expect representatives of the conservatory and maybe even the Chinese government to greet us when we returned from Europe. But no one did. There were no flow-ers or television cameras awaiting our arrival. I had returned in tri-umph; my father and I had paid our way and wound up winning the top prize, surely an honor for my country. Didn't I deserve a hero's welcome?

"Don't worry," said my dad. "Our prize money will enable us to pay back our relatives and the bank with enough left over to buy some high-end audio equipment so you can listen and learn from CDs. Everyone who knows you is proud of you. But don't expect much from the conservatory. The conservatory is a great institution of learn-ing, but it is also a hotbed of jealousy. You've seen that before, but be prepared to see it again."

But how, after reaching such great heights, could I be prepared to be dragged back down to earth?

A few months after our trip to Germany, I auditioned for the mid-dle school sector of the conservatory. I played the Hungarian Rhapsody no. 6 with great flair. Or at least I thought I did. The judges, as if to teach me my place, ranked me third. The boy who placed first had played an easy Chinese folk song. It was Professor Angry and her allies who had kept me from the top slot, and they justified their actions with a litany of criticisms about my performance. But behind all that osten-sibly well-reasoned criticism lay their real sentiments: *the European judges may have the freedom to overrate you, but here in China we will put you in your place.*

When the rankings were posted, my dad exploded. Still simmer-ing at the conservatory's snubbing me when I came home from Ettlin-gen, he boiled over at this unjust defeat. He screamed at the judges, "You have it out for my son! You know he's number one. He was num-ber one in Ettlingen against players from all over the world. He beat Yu and Zhe, the best in China. If he can beat them, he can certainly beat anyone auditioning for the middle school. And he did! You know he did! He was number one and you gave him number three only to humiliate him and let him know that you are the bosses here and what happens in Europe doesn't make any difference. In Europe the judges were fair. Here you push your own students so you can push your own careers and some take bribes! It's an outrage! An absolute outrage!"

My father also blamed Professor Zhao as much as anyone else. According to my father, Professor Angry was the one who argued against me, but Professor Zhao should have fought *for* me.

"He needed to defend you," said Dad, "but he didn't."

My father arranged for me to meet Yin Chengzong, perhaps the most famous pianist in China. He was a national star who had played only Chinese music on the piano during the Cultural Revolution. He had even been close to Madame Mao. But after the Revolution, when he fell out of favor, he had fled to the United States and made New York his permanent home. When Dad met him, he had come back to China for an extended stay, having regained his lost status in his native country.

Yin Chengzong was a Russian scholar; he spoke the language flawlessly and had mastered Russia's approach to piano, a rich, grand sound with big phrasings and hot-hearted emotions. It was as if he had the soul of a Russian. When he heard me play, he said that I, too, understood Rachmaninoff and Tchaikovsky, and he encouraged me to master those composers' most difficult pieces, which I took as the highest form of praise.

Yin Chengzong was encouraging and patient, and when he agreed to give me lessons, my father and I were elated. But we also realized that Professor Zhao couldn't know about it. He'd be incensed. Chinese teachers don't like sharing their students, and we didn't want to risk losing Professor Zhao even though my father found him cowardly. In his own way, Zhao was still an ally, so I took lessons from Yin Chengzong in secret.

When my mother came to Beijing for a short visit, I told her that I felt strange about these clandestine lessons.

"I can understand that, Lang Lang," she said, "but you aren't doing anything wrong. Sometimes teachers don't get along with each other, but all that matters is that you learn everything you need to learn because that's what music's all about."

I wished my mother could have come along with me to the competitions, but the cost was prohibitive, not to mention the difficulty of getting a visa. My father now had his sights on the International Tchaikovsky Competition for Young Musicians in Japan, which was held in the summer. It was the most difficult one of all for a young pianist, and despite the impossibility I begged my mother to come. She told me again, as she had over the years, that it was because of her love for me that she stepped aside to let my father help me become Number One, that the three of us were united in this great adventure to cultivate my talent and bring me fame, and that each of us had a role to play in this endeavor. Looking back, I now realize that of all the egos that were hitched to my career, my mother's was the most controlled. When she was forced to give up living with her son, she did so without bitterness. During her infrequent trips to Beijing, she never bemoaned her fate or complained about her difficult life. She loved me without concern for her own well-being. I, in turn, loved her even more, and during those endless years when I was practicing eight, nine, and ten hours a day, I never stopped feeling the pain of her absence. My heart cried for her. I continued to cry for my mother throughout my entire childhood and, to be honest, long after that.

Egos, teachers, contests. My childhood was wound up in all three. And my father, the world's most determined man, could not be deterred from his mission to make sure that they all worked in my favor.

"This Tchaikovsky contest in Japan is huge," he said. "Much bigger than Germany. The top six finalists will play with the Moscow Philharmonic. And the top three finalists will appear on international television. When you place first in Japan, you will be recognized all over the world. You will be offered scholarships to schools in the United States like Juilliard and Curtis. Our problems will be over. That's why we must get the best advice from the best teachers."

Professor Zhao thought I should play Mozart, but at that point my Mozart wasn't very good. I hadn't begun to understand the intricacy of his genius. I was too heavy-handed for Mozart, and I still hadn't come to fully understand the many personalities of his music. Yin Chengzong thought I should play Beethoven, which I much preferred. But my father felt that the Chopin Concerto no. 2 would show off my greatest skills, so he had me prepare that piece. And as if all these differing opinions weren't confusing enough, still another teacher got involved, the woman my dad considered the finest piano instructor in the entire country, Professor Tu, the only judge representing China in the competition.

Her fee was astronomical—one hundred dollars for a single lesson—but my dad was willing to pay, just to get another perspective. In the Chinese world of classical music, her judgment had great authority.

She asked me to play the Chopin Concerto no. 2. I was certain she'd be impressed.

"It's a mistake to play this piece in Japan," she said when I finished.

"Will you at least help him interpret it better?" my dad asked.

"No, it's the wrong selection. He doesn't understand the poetic longing that informs Chopin. He's too young, too immature for such an emotionally taxing piece. It's too romantic for a young boy."

"But—" my father began to protest.

"No 'buts' about it," Professor Tu insisted. "I'll give you your hundred dollars back. I'm simply not interested in instructing your son if he's going to perform this piece. If he does so, he won't stand a chance of winning."

My father and I looked at each other. This was serious.

"Play the Chopin, Lang Lang," said Dad once she had left.

"Are you sure?" It seemed a reckless idea.

"These teachers have always underestimated you. This one is no different."

"But what about being too young to understand the emotions of Chopin?"

"Chopin was longing for a lost love. When you play the concerto, think about the love you feel for your mother. You're always saying how you miss her. Well, put that feeling into the music."

I had never practiced in that way before, and even though I practiced like crazy, and though my longing for my mother made my heart ache, I couldn't figure out how to bring that longing to the keyboard.

When Mom came to visit a couple of months before Dad and I were scheduled to leave for Japan, she and Professor Zhao had words. My teacher made the mistake of complaining to her about Dad.

"You must control Lang Guoren," he urged her. "You must keep him away from the conservatory. His attitude is alienating everyone. He argues with the piano teachers at school, he rants and raves, and he's hurting your son's chances of getting ahead."

"My son," said Mom with a steeliness I'd never heard in her before, "seems to be getting ahead pretty well."

"He gets ahead in spite of your husband."

"He needs his father's protection. Other families have money to buy fancy gifts for their teachers. All we have is our desire to make sure our son isn't overlooked."

"Lang Guoren is certainly making sure of that. He thinks of nothing and no one but your son. Night and day, he's obsessed with Lang Lang's career."

"I'm glad. I wish you would be the same way. I wish you would protect Lang Lang when the other teachers say bad things about him."

"I'm afraid you don't understand the art of being politic."

"You're right; I don't know about that. All I know is that your conservatory has some backbiters and hypocrites."

"Be that as it may," Professor Zhao continued, "your husband is an irritant. His interference is intolerable. His involvement with your son's repertoire, for example, is uninformed and counterproductive. In this upcoming competition in Japan, do not expect Lang Lang to place higher than third. The truth is that he'll be fortunate to do that well."

"Don't believe him," said my father when Mom reported her conversation with Professor Zhao. "Don't believe anyone who says Lang Lang will not be Number One."

Hearing Professor Zhao's words, though, did have an impact on me. After all, he had been my champion. He had taken me on after Professor Angry, had seen me triumph in Germany. If he didn't believe I could win in Japan, maybe he knew something we didn't.

When my mother saw that I was anxious, she said, "You need to come home for a while, Lang Lang. Come home to Shenyang." My mom insisted that Shenyang would do me a world of good. I would take lessons from Professor Zhu, the one teacher we all trusted and loved.

I thought Dad would protest, but he didn't. "Maybe that's not a bad idea, Zhou Xiulan. Maybe it would be good for Lang Lang to see Professor Zhu."

The minute the train pulled in to the Shenyang station, I felt relief. I was home. Shenyang may not be Paris or Vienna, but to me, especially in those days before the Tchaikovsky competition in Japan, it was the most beautiful city in the world. It was summertime, and the joy of being with my mother and the nourishment of her delicious meals revived my spirit. And I was thrilled to be reunited with my beloved Professor Zhu.

In the five and a half years since I'd been away, nothing had changed in her studio. She had the same piano, the same lamps and pictures on the wall; her manner was patient as ever, her instruction compassionate.

I told her about the controversy surrounding the Chopin concerto, how famous teachers had doubts about whether I could—or should—perform it. After I played it for her, she spoke without a moment's hesitation. "I agree with your father, Lang Lang. You can play this piece, and you can play it well. But yes, you must feel the longing and the pain. You must express these deep emotions without fear or embarrassment. This is a composition where you must reach down to your depths and find the meaning for yourself. Now play it again."

I played it again, this time remembering that my visit to Shenyang was temporary, that once again I'd be far from my mother's embrace and Professor Zhu's kind instruction, and that grief seemed to guide my fingers over the keys.

When I looked up, there were tears in Professor Zhu's eyes.

"You can play this piece," she said. "I am certain that you can play it."

A week later, in August 1995, my dad, Professor Zhao, and I were in Sendai, Japan. I now had a blue passport; the government was paying for my trip. The first thing I saw in the Japanese newspaper was a photograph of a young girl, about my age, standing in front of a grand piano.

"Who is she?" I asked Professor Zhao.

"The best student piano player in this country. She is a brilliant Japanese girl. The media here love her. No doubt she will win," he answered matter-of-factly.

His words crushed me.

I carefully examined the picture: her eyes were clear, her hands delicate. I imagined those slender fingers flying over the keys.

"Do you know what she'll be playing?" I asked.

"I don't," said my teacher. "But it hardly matters. She's the clear favorite."

Later my father learned that the second favorite was a girl from Ukraine who had placed second in the previous competition held in Moscow three years earlier.

"We must watch them both practice," said Dad, "and study their techniques." We had a week to conduct our research.

When I found out where they were practicing, I made my way over to their rooms. Their doors were partially open, so I could peek in and see how they moved their fingers and phrased the music. They were powerful players. I studied them for a long time until a reporter from one of the newspapers covering the Japanese girl came by and asked what I was doing. When I told him, he laughed and took notes for his story. Maybe he would write something bad about me, but I didn't care. I needed to hear the players for myself. That way I'd be even more motivated to beat them.

The Tchaikovsky was far bigger than any contest I'd ever entered. The hotel where we stayed flew forty flags representing all the countries that had sent students to compete. After the first round, only twenty flags were flying. China had sent ten of us, and we all made the first cut. But it was the second cut that was critical—forty contestants would be narrowed down to six.

The Chinese boy who had placed first in the middle school auditions where I placed third had come to Japan brimming with confidence. "I'm number one," he kept telling whoever would listen. But when the list following the second round was posted, his name was not there. In fact, I was the only representative of China that made it to the top six. The others were two Russians, an English girl, the girl from

Japan, and the girl from Ukraine. All six of us were to play with the Moscow Philharmonic, which was thrilling, except for one thing—I'd never played with an orchestra before. Back in Beijing, my dad had asked Professor Zhao to arrange rehearsals with a Chinese orchestra, but Zhao had told us that would cost nearly two thousand dollars. We didn't have anywhere near that much money.

"Can you help us?" my father asked Professor Zhao.

"Not if you don't have the money."

I was going in cold.

"Think of your mother," my father told me. "Think of how she loves you. Think of how you miss her. Think of what she means to you. Put your love and longing for her into the Chopin. Don't think about anyone or anything else. Play for your mother, Lang Lang. Play for Zhou Xiulan."

With my mother in mind, I managed to quickly adapt to the sounds and rhythms of the orchestra behind me. In this way, though she was countless miles away, my mother was beside me now, filling the space left behind by my childhood heroes. As I played, I put my longing for her into the second movement, and I found a breathing poetry of loneliness that I'd never felt before when I played. The Moscow Philharmonic sounded fabulous. I loved every second of playing with an orchestra. It seemed like once you had an orchestra, you had wings.

When the winners were announced, I was resigned to the fact that I had done all I could do. At least I was in the top six, an accomplishment in and of itself.

Number six was England.

Number five was Ukraine.

Number four was Russia.

I was in the top three. My father later confessed he hadn't thought I'd make it that far, since all the video cameras were pointing at players from Russia and Japan.

Number three was also Russia.

It was down to me and the Japanese girl, the media darling, the one that Professor Zhao said no one could beat. So, I thought, I had made number two. For the first time I imagined I could live with second place.

Then came the word.

Number two . . . I closed my eyes, held my breath, and when the voice called out the name, it was not mine, it was the Japanese girl's!

I shot up; I was so excited I was shaking. As my name was announced, I waved my arms. I was number one.

"I knew you'd be number one," Professor Zhao said. "I just knew it."

I didn't say anything to him. Neither did my dad. There was nothing to say except "Thank you."

One of the judges whispered in my ear, "There was sunshine in your playing, Lang Lang, bright and glorious sunshine."

Many of my competitors came to me crying, saying I had touched them. I was very moved by their encouragement and wished them the best in their playing.

Flashbulbs began popping and reporters gathered around me. They asked for my reaction.

"I am honored," I said. "I feel very lucky because the other contestants were so good."

"What is your next contest?" they asked.

"I don't know," I answered.

"What I do know," my father said later when we were alone, "is that after this great victory, Lang Lang, your life will never be the same."

The Battle
of Rachmaninoff

When I returned to Beijing, not only was my mother waiting for me at the airport, but so was the president of the music conservatory and the press. I was receiving the kind of attention reserved for superstars in sports or film, the kind of attention I'd always fantasized about, what I'd wished for when I returned from Germany. I was flying. My feet never touched the ground. At the Beijing Concert Hall, I played the complete twenty-four études by Chopin, and the critics raved. I was thirteen.

Almost every week a major article about me was printed in the papers. I had finally become king of the conservatory, but, strangely, Professor Zhao seemed to be competing with me for the title. He courted the press and claimed credit for all of my achievements, even the special merit of distinction in Germany. According to Zhao, it was he who had insisted I play the Chopin Concerto no. 2, he who had discovered and nurtured my talent, he who was planning my future.

At around the same time, professors from the music conservatory were preparing a New Year's program for national television featuring their best students. Zhai, the boy I had called Master of the North Region and one of the protégés of Professor Zhao's wife, Professor Ling, was also to appear. Once, he had been the most famous young pianist in China, but I had replaced him. Yet when we arrived at the television studio, I discovered that Professor Ling had given Zhai the piece I was set to play.

"That's unacceptable," my father said. "And unfair."

"Who are you to make such statements?" asked Professor Ling. "You are nothing but a parent. We are the professors."

"You have given Zhai the composition that Lang Lang has prepared. Why would you do that?"

"What we do and don't do is our professional business. You are an amateur and don't understand these things."

"But, Professor—," said my dad before she cut him off and started to scream, right there in front of the cameramen and directors.

"Get this man off the set! I'll have nothing to do with him! Security! See to it that you remove this man from the studio at once!"

Her tirade inspired a new ferocity in me; my whole life I'd been the dutiful, deferential pupil, but now it was time to fight on my father's behalf just as he had fought for me all those years.

"If he goes," I said, "I go."

My ultimatum shocked Professor Ling out of her hysterics.

"And what's more," I added, "if I don't get to play the piece I prepared, I'll go anyway."

Her mouth twisted to form any number of protests, but there was nothing she could say.

The next thing I knew, the television director was conferring with Professor Zhao and his wife. I heard them arguing among themselves. Finally, they approached me.

"Okay, Lang Lang," they said. "Perform the piece you prepared. Zhai will find something else to play."

And just like that, the battle between Professor Zhao and me ended. I emerged the victor.

■

"It is high time for Lang Lang to play Rachmaninoff's Third Piano Concerto," my father told Professor Zhao some weeks later. The three of us were at the professor's office in the conservatory, planning my future.

"No," said the professor. "He isn't ready. Those Rachmaninoff pieces are far too difficult. They'll just frustrate him."

"He'll master them in no time," said my father.

"He'll mangle them. He must wait. The conservatory has a certain system that we must follow. We have a prescribed plan of study, and Rachmaninoff doesn't come till later."

"I don't care about your school rules," said Dad.

"Well, I do," the teacher insisted.

"When it comes to learning music, when has Lang Lang ever followed the school rules?" my father asked. "He has always made a curriculum of his own."

"He has always followed *my* curriculum."

"Perhaps in the past, but not in the future," said my father. "There is a Greek piano prodigy who debuted at Carnegie Hall at the age of thirteen playing Rach's Third, and if he could do it, Lang Lang can do it, too. Besides, we've been invited to New York by Yin Chengzong."

"I forbid it. Lang Lang is *my* student, not Yin Chengzong's."

"Lang Lang is *my* son, Professor Zhao, not yours."

"Are you sure we're doing the right thing?" I asked my dad. "If Professor Zhao is angry with us, we'll have no one at the conservatory on our side."

"Now that you are playing onstage, you need to study classical music in the West. You need to see the world," said my father. "We must go to America and find the best teachers there."

"Why not Europe? Why not Germany?" I asked, remembering the beauty, the food, the hospitality.

"Europe has many wonderful teachers, but launching your career as a concert pianist will be easier from America. America is not as traditional or stodgy as Europe. America is more open to new ideas and new artists. America has great music conservatories and great teachers."

"But where will the money come from?" I asked.

"America. America is the richest country in the world."

AMERICA

America

Carnegie Hall and Michael Jordan—these were the two things I wanted to see most in America. I didn't get to see Michael Jordan, who was probably as famous in China as he was in the United States, but I did find myself standing in front of Carnegie Hall. Yin Chengzong had arranged a recital for me at Steinway Hall on Fifty-seventh Street, and Carnegie Hall was just a block away. My father and I arrived for my performance an hour early, and when I learned that the famous concert venue was so close, I decided to walk down the street to see it for myself.

I fell in love with New York at first sight. The city pulsated; its rhythms excited me. The skyscrapers, all crowded together, seemed to compete with each other. So did the people on the streets. A competitor myself, I was drawn into this maze of urban contests. Who can walk the fastest? Who can make the most money? From the top of the Empire State Building I could see to the very ends of the world. I wandered around Rockefeller Center, and got lost in the great green expanse of Central Park. But it was Carnegie Hall, the heaven for music, that temple of temples, that symbolized everything I wanted from this great city.

By chance, a door was open and I was able to slip inside. A man was vacuuming the lobby, but he ignored me as I found my way into the hall itself. My heart pounding, I thought of those who had played there. Primarily, I thought of the two men I most idolized: Arthur Rubinstein and Vladimir Horowitz. I thought of them sitting on the stage before me, playing for an audience of devotees enraptured by their every phrase. At that moment, I dreamed of the day that I would play a solo recital on this sacred ground. As Isaac Stern said in a movie I once saw, when you play at Carnegie Hall, every great musician will listen to you, for their spirits are there.

Make it come true, I prayed to the gods, the muses, and whatever other mystical powers might have influence over the course of human events.

Later that day, I was back in Steinway Hall, itself an imposing architectural structure, an immense round room covered with oil paintings of every important figure in the history of the piano. I felt their eyes on me, so it was no wonder I was nervous. Yin Chengzong had invited a large group of prominent critics and educators to listen to me play my first American concert. He introduced me as a young star with a bright future. In this vast metropolis, where my heroes had performed, I suddenly worried that this impartial audience would not agree with him. Before I walked to the piano, my dad, sensing my apprehension, gave me his traditional pat on the back, the pat that infused me with courage.

As I performed before those important people whose language I still did not understand, my fear dissipated. I repeated the program of Chopin's twenty-four études that had won over the audience in Beijing, and the magic worked again.

Yin Chengzong reported glowing reviews from nearly everyone in attendance. "Very shortly," he told my father, "we should have offers of scholarships from several different institutions. That will enable

Lang Lang to remain in America, find management, and launch his career."

I had won a scholarship to a summer music camp in Walnut Hill, some twenty miles west of Boston, where Yin Chengzong taught. The camp broadened my horizons in ways beyond musical instruction. I learned to swim and found freedom in the feeling of gliding through water. Tennis was another revelation. Whacking that small furry ball back and forth over a net brought me unexpected pleasure, more so even than Ping-Pong. Pretending I was Michael Jordan shooting jump shots on the basketball court fed my crazy fantasy of playing in the NBA. For a whole month I did what normal teens do during the summer—walk through the woods, dive in a lake, play ball. And of course there was lots of practice, too, and trying to learn English.

The highlight of camp was a field trip into the Berkshires, where the Tanglewood Music Festival, situated in a pastoral setting of great beauty, introduced me to the talents of André Watts, the internationally acclaimed pianist who, a few years later, would change the course of my life.

Another trip took us into Boston, where we spent a day at the Museum of Fine Arts. I was awestruck at the size of the collection and the variety of the represented cultures—ancient, modern, American, European, and Asian. I stood before Paul Gauguin's *Where Do We Come From? What Are We? Where Are We Going?* and pondered its erotic mystery. I fell in love with Monet. I delighted in the great paintings of Titian, Rembrandt, Renoir, and van Gogh. They transported me back in time and allowed me to understand the very nature of art, its wild passions and extravagant beauty.

The entire experience of this New England summer was wonderful except for one thing: the constant presence of my dad. Normally kids shared a room with each other. I shared a room with him. The other kids were on their own, but I had my father by my side, making sure I didn't miss a day of practice. In fact, at the end of camp, Dad was asked if I would play a recital for elderly people at a nursing home. The pay was two hundred dollars, and I was more than willing to perform. I decided to give it my all and treat the audience to the twenty-four Chopin études. They were thrilled, and at the end of the concert I was exhausted. Surely my effort entitled me to a day off.

"No," said my father. "No day off. The Americans can afford to miss a practice session, but you can't. Tomorrow you'll put in your four hours like any other day."

And I did.

Meanwhile, in spite of Yin Chengzong's efforts, no one had offered me a scholarship to study full-time at an American school.

"It'll take just a bit more time," said Yin Chengzong. "Please be patient."

But I had tasted America, and I wanted more. I was out of school and out of sorts; my life was caught between West and East.

Then everything changed when a telegram arrived from China. My first thought was that Mom was ill. "What's wrong?" I demanded.

"Nothing. Nothing at all. Everything is right! We must hurry and make arrangements," my father replied.

"Arrangements for what?"

"Our return to China."

"When?"

"Today, tomorrow, as soon as possible."

"But why? Why must we leave? I like it here!"

I had been asked to perform for President Jiang Zemin of China as the featured soloist at the inaugural concert of the China National Symphony Orchestra, which would be broadcast on national television.

"We must hurry home," my father told me. "You must start practicing immediately."

"And America?" I asked him.

"You'll be back, Lang Lang. You'll be back before you know it."

Farewell

On September 6, 1996, at the age of fourteen, I played Beethoven's Choral Fantasy before the president of my country at the inauguration concert of China's first full-time orchestra in history, the China National Symphony Orchestra, which had previously been known as the Central Philharmonic Orchestra of China. It was a grand occasion. The audience was packed with the most illustrious dignitaries in the worlds of art, culture, and business. I had never played the piece before and had been given only a week to practice it.

"Now you too are a dignitary, Lang Lang," my mother told me in the dressing room while helping me with my tux. "You are an important person in the culture of our country."

Her words helped settle my stomach, but it was Dad's pat on the back that set me in motion and had me playing with a poise that surprised even me. The president was gracious afterward. "You are a brilliant boy," he said, "and you represent our nation admirably."

Because of my growing fame, the head of the conservatory was urging me to stay in China and continue my studies at the conservatory. They even offered to get a foreign teacher just for me. But my father and I didn't want to insult Professor Zhao, and we still had our eyes on America. After winning the Tchaikovsky contest in Japan, I also won a recording contract with the Japanese recording company JVC Victor. While making my first record, I met a woman who was friends with a Mr. Yeh, an orchestra conductor living in Indiana. Mr. Yeh knew Gary Graffman, the great concert pianist who was then president of the Curtis Institute of Music in Philadelphia, and sent him a video-tape of my performance of Chopin's Concerto no. 2 with the Moscow Philharmonic and a tape of me playing all twenty-four of Chopin's études at the Beijing Concert Hall.

Mr. Graffman was intrigued. "Where is this boy?" he asked Mr. Yeh.

Mr. Yeh explained that I had just been in America, but now was back in China. Mr. Graffman told him to find me immediately. He wanted me to audition for Curtis as soon as possible.

I not only knew Gary Graffman's work as one of the world's leading pianists and piano teachers; I also knew he had been a student of Horowitz's. To be taught by someone who had been taught by Horowitz—what more could I ask for? I was thrilled. But first, of course, I would have to audition; Mr. Graffman loved my tape, but his school required an in-person performance. Although Mr. Graffman couldn't have been more encouraging, there were no guarantees.

"You will not fail," my father assured me. "You have faced far more challenging situations than this. You pulled off the impossible in Germany and Japan, and, believe me, you will knock the Curtis Institute's socks off!"

A date was set. I would go back to America.

But what about Mom? What if I won the scholarship and wound up living abroad? Could Mom come too?

My mother told me I would have to go without her. She was still afraid to give up her job—my future was not yet secure.

"I might be there for years. I don't know when I'll be coming back," I told her.

"Look how quickly the years have passed since you went to Beijing. Look at all the good things that have happened to you. Good things will happen in America as well, and you'll be back in China before you know it."

I knew her words were true; there was no arguing with her logic. If I had to study at a music school in a foreign country, my father needed to be there with me.

It was March 1997. Although my chance of gaining admission to Curtis was excellent, the school was not prepared to pay for our trip, so that money was coming out of Mom's salary. The cash prizes we had won in the past had gone to pay off debts. We were still broke, and buying round-trip tickets to America meant borrowing more from our friends and relatives.

When I arrived in Philadelphia, the city was covered in a soft blanket of snow. It made the campus of the famous Curtis Institute of Music, where Rudolf Serkin had once been president and whose former students included Leonard Bernstein, Gian Carlo Menotti, and Samuel Barber, seem all the more enchanted.

The school was housed in imposing mansions in Center City, Philadelphia, on Rittenhouse Square, the most historic section of the city. Each building had been lovingly preserved; the Oriental rugs, woodwork, and antique furniture were magnificent, and to walk among it all felt like stepping back in time. As my father and I were escorted to Mr. Graffman's office, I felt as if I were traveling into early U.S. history, when the Americans were fighting the English for their independence. Unlike the hustle and bustle of modern New York, Philadelphia felt older and calmer.

Mr. Graffman was one of the most cordial men I had ever met. He greeted me and my dad in Mandarin. Among other things, he was an expert in Chinese culture. His office was filled with Chinese paintings, Chinese sculpture, Chinese calligraphy, and rare artifacts from the ancient Chinese dynasties. He knew more about my country's history than I did and instantly put me at ease.

He said, "Today I just want to give you a little lesson and help you prepare for tomorrow's audition. I understand that you'll be playing the Beethoven sonatas opus 110 and Bach's preludes and fugues."

"Yes."

"Well, that's wonderful. I know you'll do splendidly. Now, if you wouldn't mind, let's start with Beethoven."

As I played, I felt that he wasn't judging me but was, rather, appreciating me. He wasn't looking for what I did wrong but was acknowledging what I did right. When I was through, he had comments about certain phrasings, but he presented them as suggestions rather than commands. He was gentle, and in that sense he reminded me of Professor Zhu. He motivated not by fear but with love—love of the music, love of his protégés, love of the very act of teaching. I had never studied with a world-class performer before, and from the first moment I could sense his strong pianistic skills.

"Tomorrow," he said, "you will no doubt be impressed by those who will be listening to your audition."

I noticed how he said "listening," not "judging."

"Who will be there?" I asked.

"Leon Fleisher, Claude Frank, Seymour Lipkin, and Peter Serkin."

At the mention of all these major figures in the world of classical piano my face must have registered concern, for Mr. Graffman rushed to reassure me. "These men will be impressed by your virtuosity and musicianship. Your job is to relax and simply enjoy the music that you play. I intend to enjoy it as well."

"I'm sure we will all enjoy Lang Lang's playing," said my father.

"Unfortunately, Lang Guoren," Mr. Graffman responded, "parents are not allowed in the hall during the auditions."

We were staying at the lovely home of an American family in

Center City, and that night, as I slept with my father's arm around me, I dreamed of snowstorms in faraway lands. I dreamed of Michael Jordan hitting his jump shot and winning the championship. I dreamed of Chinese Olympic gymnastic teams winning gold medals.

When I awoke, the city was still white. At age fourteen, I had won many big contests, but I knew this audition was the most important test of my abilities. My father had stressed the importance of getting an American musical education. He said, "America is the most open country with the most possibilities. In America, the sky is the limit."

When we arrived at the main mansion that houses Curtis, we found other students waiting in the lobby. My dad's English was non-existent and mine was poor, so we didn't understand the organizers of the audition when they gave instructions. Then another stroke of good luck occurred. A young Chinese man appeared.

"May I help you?" he asked.

"Yes, please," said my father. "We don't know what we are being told."

"Are you from northern China?"

"Yes," I said. "Are you?"

"Yes, your accents give you away."

Ge Qun Wang, who told me he was called GQ in America, after the famous magazine, introduced himself as an opera student. He directed me to the second floor, where the auditions were taking place, but told my father he was not allowed to accompany me. Twenty minutes later, just as I was about to walk into the audition room, I saw GQ running after me. "Your father asked me to come up here and pat you on the back and tell you that you're Number One."

In the room sat a panel of the most distinguished judges I had ever encountered—Graffman, Serkin, Fleisher, Frank, Lipkin. But I wasn't afraid. I was exhilarated to show these brilliant artists how long and how diligently I had practiced the music they loved most.

"You played so well," said Mr. Graffman two hours later. "You were the best of all the applicants." He told me I had won a full scholarship, an apartment with a Steinway grand piano in the living room, and living expenses.

When I told my dad, he didn't believe me. "Are you sure your English is good enough to have understood the man?" he asked.

"He told me in Chinese."

"Tell me again. I can't believe it."

The news was so intense that my father had to sit down on the bed to take it in. He could barely breathe. At first we thought my father's shortened breath was just an emotional reaction to our good news, but the next day, on the plane back to China, it was clear that something was seriously wrong with him. Halfway through the trip, he was gasping for air, and I became alarmed. I told the stewardess, who said she would alert the airport in Beijing to have an ambulance waiting for us upon our arrival.

Mom was waiting as well. She congratulated me on my scholarship, but my good news was quickly overshadowed by Dad's medical emergency. When we got to the hospital, doctors X-rayed his throat and found two large tumors. They were unable to tell us whether it was cancer or how grave a threat it was, but they told us we could not visit my father; the temptation to talk would be too great, and talking would only worsen the problem.

I didn't want to leave my father. I couldn't imagine what life would be like without him. For all the misery he had caused me, for all his strictness and militaristic manners, I knew how much I needed him, and I knew how much he wanted to come to America to help me fulfill our dream. I realized for the first time how much I loved him. He simply couldn't die.

Those were dark days. I cried all the time; at night, my mother held me in her arms while I sobbed myself to sleep. "It will be fine, Lang Lang," she said. "Your father will pull through. He's a strong man." But her words didn't comfort me. Without my father, what would become of me?

Fortunately, the tumors were not cancerous and could be removed without complications. But his hospital stay would be a long one.

"I'll visit you every day," I told my father.

"I don't want you visiting," he said. "I want you practicing."

After the operation, when he was finally released, he was fine— except that he couldn't speak for a month. I didn't mind that. I could talk to him, and for once he couldn't talk back.

In order to communicate, he scribbled down words on scraps of paper. One afternoon, while we were discussing our final months in China, he wrote, "We should do something big. We should leave China with a bang."

"How?" I asked out loud.

He thought for a moment, and then wrote two words:

"Farewell tour."

Beijing 9, Shanghai 1

My father had survived a grave threat to his life. My mother had survived living without her son and husband for seven years. I had survived a crazy life of competition with an even crazier father by my side, berating me even as he comforted me. As a family, we were divided in many ways, but we were also united; we were bonded by blood and by our dedication to furthering my musical education—what was now becoming my professional musical career.

The farewell tour began in Beijing and included Shanghai, the commercial center of China, where I was little known, with stops along the way in Xi'an, Dalian, Changchun, and Harbin. There was enough interest that my father decided to book a few select concerts for which I would be paid. Even before starting school in the United States, I had become a professional.

My dad saw Shanghai as the ultimate conquest. In his mind, I had triumphed in Beijing, where I played before the president and received glowing notices. But Shanghai was different; it was the pinnacle of Chinese taste and refinement, and it boasted a great conservatory. Many of my previous rivals had trained there. The people there viewed themselves as *the* connoisseurs of classical music, and according to my dad's plan, if I could win over the skeptics in Shanghai, I could leave China in a blaze of glory.

These last concerts were just recitals because the cost of performing with an orchestra was too great, and besides, my father reasoned, the people wanted to see me, a young boy, alone onstage. The people of Shanghai, though, were quick to complain about the steep ticket prices. "Who is this kid?" they asked. "And why should he demand top price for a recital?" But despite their doubts, they were curious, and the concert was sold out.

It was a tumultuous day, one that must be seen in the context of an ancient geographic rivalry within China between north and south. Of course my loyalties, as a northerner from Shenyang, were with Beijing. I had been told that people from Shanghai look down on Beijingers as hicks. So as a soccer fanatic I was particularly pleased that on the very day of my last concert, in a grudge match between Shanghai and Beijing, Beijing won 9 to 1. I watched the game with unrestrained joy. We had walloped them! And if our boys could beat them so easily in soccer, then I could do the same on the piano. When I reached the hall that night, I was inspired, determined to be unforgettable.

I was on that night. The Beethoven sonatas, the Mozart sonatas, all the Chopin études, Liszt's Hungarian Rhapsodies—it was a huge program that, even in its first few moments, won over the audience. By the time it ended, the good people of Shanghai were on their feet and shouting. We had won for the second time that day.

The following afternoon I posed with the Beijing soccer team for a picture that was plastered across the front pages of the Shanghai papers.

The concert in Shanghai was most important to my father, but my final concert in China, in my home city of Shenyang, meant even more to me. There I would play before my teachers—including Professor Zhu—my relatives, and a city of friends. I would not have to win over the people of Shenyang as I had done in Shanghai. Shenyang had loved and supported me from the start.

I was looking forward to the long train trip home because my parents and I were traveling as a family. I sat next to Mom on the train and told her of my excitement and apprehension about this pending move to America. She listened with her heart, as she always does, understanding all my conflicting emotions and comforting me. We had been talking for more than an hour when my dad, sitting across the aisle, came over to us, fuming.

"That's enough!"

"Enough of what, Lang Guoren?" my mother asked.

"Enough talking with Lang Lang."

"Why shouldn't Lang Lang talk to his mother, Lang Guoren?"

"Because he should be studying his English and studying the scores of the pieces he has to play in Shenyang."

"It's important that Lang Lang and I have this time together," said Mom. "God knows how long we'll be separated. He won't be back from America for years."

"He still has to study."

"A normal boy needs to spend time with his mother."

"Our son is not a normal boy. You are wasting his time, Zhou Xiulan."

"Wasting his time! You call loving my son a waste of time?"

"Stop complaining. Let the boy be. You weaken his resolve by coddling him. You think you're helping him, but you're hurting him."

With that, my mother started to cry. She wept quietly; she tried restraining her tears so I wouldn't be upset, but she couldn't stop crying. Of the three of us, she had been the strongest, enduring endless stretches of loneliness all for my benefit, and now my father wanted to rob her of the precious little time she had before I stepped entirely out of her reach.

"I want to stay here next to Mom," I insisted.

"I don't care what you want," my dad retorted.

He yanked me out of my seat and threw me down in the seat next to him. "Here's your English workbook," he said. "Here are your scores. Start studying."

There is a famous Chinese folk song called "My Country" whose emotions I had never been able to express; to be honest, I never liked it. I didn't understand the meaning behind it, and I certainly didn't feel it. It's an old song from my grandparents' time, and the melody is tinged with an inward-looking sadness that seemed distant from my own experience. But on the night of my Shenyang farewell, I connected to the piece as I never had before. I found that sadness within my own soul. As I played "My Country," the excitement I'd been feeling about beginning a new life in the land of opportunity receded. I would be leaving my country—my city, my family, my mother. My eyes filled with tears as the song said, in stark, simple terms, goodbye.

At the gala reception afterward, my early childhood in Shenyang passed before me as I greeted old friends and friends of my parents. It was a lovely occasion that I wanted to share with my mother, but I couldn't find her. I asked everyone where she had gone, but no one could tell me. I began to worry. What could have happened that my mother wouldn't be at my farewell party?

"Where has Mom gone?" I asked my dad when I'd finally found him. "Why isn't she here? Everyone is asking for her."

"She's home," he said. "She's packing our bags for tomorrow's flight."

"That's not fair!" I said.

"If she doesn't do it," said my father, "who will?"

Going through customs, I held on to a Chinese good-luck coin that a young musician friend had thoughtfully given me. I looked up at the Chinese flag and said, "One day I will be back. And I will make you proud."

I boarded the plane, sat next to my dad, and thought about my mom.

"When will we see her next?" I asked.

"No telling," Dad said.

"A year? Two? Three?"

"Perhaps more. In America, you must buckle down and study in a new way. You have a language to learn and a career to build. That should be your main concern, not your mother."

The plane raced down the runway and lifted off, tearing through a sky of broken clouds. This would be my third trip to America, but this time it would be different. I was going to stay.

Hip-Hop

For the six years my dad and I had lived in Beijing, we had known extreme poverty. We had lived through freezing winters in heatless apartments in the city's worst neighborhoods. We owned one broken-down bike and had to scrounge for food. We begged and borrowed the money we needed to get to Germany, and when I won that prize, we were able to pay back our debts with a little left over. The Tchaikovsky victory was sweet, but it didn't relieve our economic plight. My first commercial concerts earned us enough money for plane fare to America.

It was only in America that we were able to exhale. For the first time since I started playing the piano, pressure was lifted. For the first time since we had left Shenyang, we were living above the poverty level. Curtis paid for everything—tuition, private lessons with Gary Graffman, books, living expenses, and an English tutor.

The school had even sent a car to the airport to bring us into the city. When the driver dropped us off at a high-rise building in the heart of the city, I felt as if I had stepped onto a Hollywood set. We rode the elevator to the seventh floor, walked down the hallway, and opened the door to an immaculate one-bedroom apartment equipped with central heating, central air-conditioning, our very own bathroom, and, most amazing of all, a seven-foot Steinway B piano in the living room. When I saw the Steinway, I knew I had hit the jackpot.

Our window looked right out onto the construction site for the Kimmel Center for the Performing Arts, a new concert hall for the Philadelphia Orchestra. Over the next few years, like the building, I felt my new life being constructed; I imagined my career going up, up, up.

In bed that night, my mind was overactive. I'd bounce out of bed every few minutes and run to the living room, where I would touch the Steinway, just to make sure that I wasn't dreaming. In the bed next to mine, Dad was also having a restless night. When he awoke in the morning, he looked haggard. "I dreamed I was back in the factory in Shenyang," he said. "I dreamed that none of this was real, that we never arrived in Philadelphia, that we were back in the slums of Beijing, where I had to get up at five in the morning and lock myself in the bathroom we shared with those five other families so that when you awoke you wouldn't have to wait forever to wash your hands and get ready to practice."

The architect of this new dream life was Mr. Graffman. He and his lovely wife, Naomi, treated me like a son; they invited me and Dad to dinner all the time, made certain I had a private tutor for English, and even directed Dad to a language school. For both of us, English proved to be a problem.

That's where our friend GQ was so helpful. He became the third member of our family in America. He was twenty-five, ten years older than I was and twenty years younger than Dad, so he became my older brother and Dad's younger brother. His English was perfect. He helped us with countless daily tasks—getting a phone, opening a bank account, calling the utility companies. In return, I'd accompany him as he sang for my father. GQ was a gifted singer who appreciated that my dad's critiques were always right on the money.

My dad had an especially hard time with English. He picked up some words here and there, but GQ's willingness to interpret meant Dad could slack off.

Fortunately, I couldn't do the same. Curtis's policy required that I go to a public high school for nonmusical training, and I was in for a real culture shock. With my lousy English, I was thrown into a street world of hip-hop. The first words I learned were "Ya, me," meaning "Do you know what I mean?" My first complete sentence was "What's up, dude?" and when I said it to Mr. Graffman, he responded with a smile. "My, you learn fast," he told me.

American school culture wasn't completely foreign to me. I'd had a taste of American teenage culture at music camp, and I related to the guys my age when it came to sports; I loved the 76ers basketball team and followed their every move. Still, the Philadelphia teenagers were very different from the middle-class musicians I'd met in the woods of New England. My new life was a revelation in so many ways, and perhaps the aspect that drew me in right away and made me feel at home was, surprisingly enough, rap music. I could feel the pulsating beats of the music that both the white and the black kids loved to play on their boom boxes. Rap was hypnotic. I liked the way the rappers waved their hands and jerked their heads. The relationship between the poetry and the beats intrigued me, even though I couldn't understand the poetry. I guessed it had to be about girls because that's what teenage boys like me thought about, but—at least in the beginning—I missed all the subtleties of the slang. To me, it was just raw rhythm.

The rawness of my English gave me something of a complex. I had things to say but didn't know how to say them. In the classroom, I barely understood the teacher. My tutor helped, but progress came slowly. Fortunately, compared with Chinese schools, the American system felt downright lax. Students were not disciplined, and they would think nothing about not completing their homework, which was unheard of in China. In many ways, I was ahead of the students in my class. In China, I had been terrible at math, but in America it was far less demanding and I excelled at it. English was hard, though; when I read essays by the other kids, I was amazed by their imaginations. In general, schoolwork was easy in America. It seemed that students got by doing very little.

As a fifteen-year-old boy, I didn't object to this. In fact, I liked it. I welcomed being in a country where kids were more carefree about school and independent—and even defiant—of their parents, given the domineering nature of my father, whom I'd still never truly forgiven for urging me to kill myself in our Beijing apartment. To see kids my age question authority was a revelation.

"America is so easy," I said to my father. "The homework is easy, and half the kids don't do it anyway."

"Don't get any ideas," my dad shot back. "I'm still your father and I'm still in charge. It's okay to be happy here, but don't get too happy. I'm still your boss."

There was no need to argue, and I didn't—at least not yet. In China, my dad had been in his element; every father in China raises his child with unchallenged power. But here he was a stranger in a strange land.

In school, I was dealing with two foreign languages—regular English and schoolyard English, where the favorite word was "yo." The kids, black and white, were listening to rappers with names like the Notorious B.I.G., Jay-Z, Snoop Doggy Dogg, and Puff Daddy. Everyone spoke rapidly, as if speaking the rhymes in the raps, and for months I didn't understand a word of what was said. My own musical culture, of course, was rooted in centuries past, yet I was drawn to the immediacy of the street music and the passion behind the beats. I longed to understand it better, but that wouldn't come for a long time. Meanwhile, I observed. One day some of the kids asked me what music I played, and I listed Bach, Beethoven, and Mozart. "Oh, dead man's music," they replied.

Similarly, the kids observed me. Many were kind and helpful, some even wanted to know about my background. Others expressed contempt for "the Chinese kid," calling me "Chinese Pete." I was a curiosity to them, as they were to me.

But in spite of my difficulty with English, I was a happy teenager. I was on full scholarship and out of the economic doldrums; I was attending Curtis, a fabulous school with unparalleled teachers and at least a dozen students from China; and, most important, I was in America—loose, friendly, joyful. The language would take well over a year to come to me, but the most difficult adjustment would be asked of us by the very man who had eased our transition to the States.

Gary Graffman

Ño one could question Gary Graffman's respect for Chinese culture. He understood my country as deeply as anyone I had ever met, and in fact, during many long evenings after my lessons were over, he gave me new insights into my own heritage. So I was completely unprepared when one night he urged me to reject my culture's defining values. I had prepared for him a list of contests that I wanted to enter, along with the repertoire I would play for each one: the Van Cliburn International Piano Competition, the International Tchaikovsky Competition, the Leeds International Pianoforte Competition, the Frederick Chopin International Piano Competition, the Queen Elisabeth

A LESSON WITH MR.
GRAFFMAN

Competition for Piano. "I'd like to be like Pete Sampras or Andre Agassi and win all of them," I told him.

Mr. Graffman didn't speak for a long time. "Chinese artistic culture," he finally said, "is highly competitive on every level. Everyone is ranked. Hierarchies are found in virtually every discipline—painting, dance, and of course music—and that competitive spirit has contributed to your own development, Lang Lang. No one can deny it. After all, you're here today because of your success in Japan. Had you not won the Tchaikovsky contest, you would not have been brought to my attention. But it is my firm belief that your days of participating in competitions must end."

It was as if he'd told me that my days of living and breathing were over. The more I won, the more I wanted to win, and the bigger the victories, the greater the prestige, and the quicker I'd get to forge my career as a concert pianist.

"I don't understand," I said. "What's wrong with contests?"

"They give you a particular kind of attitude. They direct your energy away from the process to the prize. And, in my view, Lang Lang, it can't be about the prize. It must be about the process."

Of course now I understand Mr. Graffman's point, but at the time it was almost impossible for me to grasp his meaning. My entire emotional apparatus was geared toward competition. It had been that way since I'd won my first contest at age five. If I were not preparing for some contest, where would I find motivation? What would be the point? This new idea was frightening to me.

When I told my father about Mr. Graffman's opinion, he was completely befuddled.

"You must have misunderstood him," said my father. "Of course he would want you to enter new contests and win new victories. How else can we get your career off the ground?"

Dad insisted on accompanying me to my next private lesson with Mr. Graffman. Those lessons were held in his beautiful apartment two hours away in New York City, on a high floor of a historic building across the street from Carnegie Hall.

To me, the apartment looked like a great museum of Chinese art; it had many rooms, all with high ceilings, long drapes, and antique chandeliers. Gary and Naomi Graffman escorted me and my dad into the elegant study, where a Steinway grand sat in the corner. Mrs. Graffman graciously served us tea before leaving us to our conversation. The talk, a mixture of Chinese and English, was candid.

"My father is a little confused," I said, "about your insistence that I not compete anymore."

"I understand that," said Mr. Graffman, "and I welcome the opportunity to discuss the matter in more depth."

"My father feels that if I were to stop competing, I would be endangering my career. No one in China takes you seriously if you go for any length of time without winning a major contest."

"That is the Chinese way. But here in America things are much different."

"Excuse me, Mr. Graffman," I interrupted, "I don't mean to be disrespectful, but what I've seen in America is no different from what I saw in China. For example, I love Michael Jordan. And he has to be number one—that's what he lives for. He loves it, and so do his fans. America is competition crazy just like China."

Mr. Graffman conceded that I was right but explained that the same did not apply to classical music—at least not as much. Although there were teachers in America who pushed their students to compete, he was not one of them. At Curtis, he explained, there were no exams, just concerts. And there was no system of ranking.

My father and I were stunned. At the conservatory in Beijing we were ranked every two months.

Mr. Graffman believed that unchecked competition caused tension and interfered with the spirit of the music. Students would direct all their energy into impressing judges instead of understanding the music. "Once you eliminate the burden of having to win, you will find yourself concentrating on aspects of your playing that you may have never considered before," he told us.

"What kinds of aspects?" I asked.

"Spiritual aspects."

Mr. Graffman told us that he was aware of the tremendous sacrifices my parents had made for me, and he commended them for their devotion. "Those sacrifices will not be in vain," he told my father. "Your son will have a long and prosperous career." He promised to set me up with a top-rated booking agent, which he said was the first step in building a career.

"And will they book him with top-rated orchestras?" my father asked. "Will he be on the A-list?"

"Not at first. At first he will be on the substitution list. When someone cancels a performance, the agency will call those on the substitution list."

"Will I be the number one substitution?"

Mr. Graffman laughed, not with derision but with kindness. "I'm afraid not at first. But you will work your way up that list."

"But this substitution business sounds like it will take forever."

"Do you admire Leonard Bernstein?"

"I love Bernstein," I said.

"Well, Bernstein, who lived in this very building, was a great mentor of mine. His career was made in 1943, when he substituted for Bruno Walter and got to conduct the New York Philharmonic at Carnegie Hall. The concert was broadcast across the country on radio, and soon Lenny became a star. Watts also became famous when he substituted for Glenn Gould."

"I didn't know that," I admitted.

"Many wonderful things will happen, Lang Lang, when you concentrate on more than just being number one. Simply concentrate on the music, not where the music will take you. Making that shift will improve the quality of your playing."

My father remained unconvinced. Our worldview had been defined by our native land, and China had a powerful and all-encompassing worldview when it came to being on top. Mr. Graffman urged us both to try a new path out of concern for my artistry. "The nurturing and development of that artistry," he told us, "depend upon subtle changes in your playing that will have a dramatic impact on your future. I know you love basketball and soccer, Lang Lang, and I know those sports inspire you to excel. But the sublime works, say, of Mozart or Liszt were not written to be the focus of a sporting event. They were written to touch the human heart. We are dealing with poetry. You are a poet of the piano, Lang Lang, and, as such, you must communicate with the human heart. Am I making sense to you?"

"I think so," I said. But I still wanted to be Number One.

A Different Paradigm

When I took my classes in advanced harmony at Curtis, I was in my element. Even though my English was still subpar, I understood the subtleties of what was being taught. Musical sensitivity got me through. Whether the intricate playfulness of Mozart or the bleak tragedy of Tchaikovsky, I intuited the emotional complexities of the compositions.

On the streets, though, it was a different story. What could be more different than the sonatas of Beethoven and the songs of the Notorious B.I.G.? In a strange way, I found both exhilarating. My love of classical music had been a constant since my birth, but now I was renewing that love in the context of Curtis. Its teaching standards were the highest, but its regulations, especially in comparison to the conservatory in China, were loose. I was able to relax. And even though hip-hop beats were frenetic, they were also relaxing. They expressed the freedom that American teens claimed as their birthright. If they wanted to express their thoughts about sex, they did so. If they wanted to criticize their government or their school or even their parents, they didn't hesitate.

I got it.

My dad didn't. He didn't have a clue about what was happening outside the world of classical music or traditional Chinese music. He might appreciate a jazz pianist like Oscar Peterson for his astounding virtuosity, but that was as far as it went, and when he decided to stop his English lessons because they weren't sinking in, he grew even more isolated, sticking close to GQ. My father was moving inward, while I was moving outward. I liked the enormous landscape of American pop. I saw that there was a relationship between, say, Allen Iverson, the brilliant point guard for the Philadelphia 76ers, and the pop star Ricky Martin. They shared a common culture that recognized and rewarded their bravura and skills. I admired that bravura; I liked the way this country saw individualism as a virtue. America's chief tradition was to passionately challenge all outmoded traditions. In China, conformity is demanded; in America, it is questioned.

I now had new eyes to see the world. At first, America seemed alarmingly different, radically brash, defiantly young. But I was different, and I was brash, and I was young, and America excited those qualities in me. If anything, America fueled my already strong ambition to break through barriers and achieve my goals. Tiger Woods, the man who, at twenty-one, was the youngest golfer to win the Masters Tournament, became my role model. I wanted to be the Tiger Woods of piano. I saw America as a country of winners, a country that understood and encouraged young people to venture where no one had ventured before.

As much as our new home exposed me to an array of different arts and attitudes, America turned my father into an observer more than a participant. He would go to Curtis and try to pick up tips for me from other classes and other teachers, but his ability to do so was extremely limited. He couldn't understand what was being said.

Meanwhile, I soaked it all in. There was not only street Philly, with its roots in old rock and roll and new rap, but also, of course, old Philly, the colonial capital where America had been founded, the City of Brotherly Love, the city of the Liberty Bell, the cradle of American democracy, the place where the Constitution took form. You can't live in Philly and not be conscious of its importance in history. Philadelphia contains all the paradoxes of America; it is a city that symbolizes the great American experiment in equality and representative government, and yet it's overrun with grinding poverty. In Philadelphia, I saw where the wealthy lived, but I also saw the homeless. Unlike our neighborhood in Beijing, Philly had streets where I feared walking alone. The city was teeming with crime.

The old culture of Philadelphia, of course, was what drew me there to begin with. Philadelphia is in the Big Five of America's great orchestras, along with New York, Chicago, Boston, and Cleveland. When President Richard Nixon took his groundbreaking trip to China in the early 1970s, the Philadelphia Orchestra, under Eugene Ormandy, joined him, becoming the first American orchestra to visit China. The musicians were received like long-lost friends; the critics raved, and to this day the Philadelphia Orchestra has a special place in the hearts of the Chinese people. In China, the Philadelphia sound is bigger than the Beatles.

There was high culture Philadelphia, classical music Philadelphia, concert hall Philadelphia, colonial Philadelphia, Revolutionary War Philadelphia, quaint Philadelphia, picturesque, elegant, stately Philadelphia.

And then there was street Philly, Allen Iverson Philly, *Big Willie Style* Philly, cheesesteak Philly, rough Philly, funky Philly.

I derived energy from both. And even if the two occupying the same space didn't make sense, that didn't matter. What mattered was being in America, where all bets were off and, much to my delight, I felt creative and alive.

I practiced six to seven hours every single day, including Sundays and holidays. But in America, it seemed, even a practice-crazed young pianist could indulge in leisure time. I went to a multiplex for the first time. I watched TV. I saw France win the World Cup—my beloved Chinese team didn't even do well enough to participate. I learned about Americans from shows like *Frasier* and *Friends* and *Sex and the City*. I was shocked to hear women speak so candidly about sex, and it motivated me even more to learn English so I could understand the racy dialogue.

My relationship with girls was progressing. I had crushes; I even had dates. Maybe because I was known at Curtis as someone who had won big international prizes, I even had a small number of female admirers. Being with girls was a wonderful diversion. But when I was on a date, walking through the park or going to the movies, it was hard not to remember the ironic title of the autobiography written by my teacher Gary Graffman: *I Really Should Be Practicing*.

"*You* really should be practicing" was my father's permanent mantra. The more he saw me acclimating to American culture and American attitudes, the stricter he became and the more resentful I became of his interference. In China, parents are in charge. In America, kids are in charge of themselves, and I was primed to assume control of my own life. Our conflicts became more frequent. Because I was number four on the substitution list compiled by the management firm Mr. Graffman set me up with, I was rarely called to concertize. This made my father nervous.

"When the call does come," he said, "you must be prepared. That means more time practicing."

"Seven hours is enough."

"Push it to nine."

"No," I said.

"Who are you to say no?"

"Who are you to tell me what to do?"

"Such insolence!"

And with that, my father threw a shoe at me. I ducked just in time.

"You'll do what I say!" he yelled at me.

"I know what I'm doing," I countered. "I'm prepared for any concert they give me."

"I don't think so."

"I know so."

"Such arrogance!"

Another shoe came at me like a rocket. This time it caught my ear. Furious, I ran out of our apartment and slammed the door behind me.

A week later I was practicing at Curtis surrounded by two or three of my Chinese friends. As he often did, Dad came by to listen. The piece I was learning was the monstrously difficult *Islamey* by Balakirev, a nineteenth-century Russian. Along with his contemporaries like Mussorgsky, Borodin, and Rimsky-Korsakov, Balakirev wrote with tremendous energy but also outlandish technical command. His work made me feel as if I needed a second pair of hands. But these were the challenges I thrived on. By the time my father arrived, I had played *Islamey* three times from start to finish, and I had played it well.

"Again," said my father.

I began to argue, but decided it would be easier to placate him than to fight. I played it again.

"And again!" my father insisted. "I heard some mistakes."

He was right. One more time wouldn't hurt me. I played the piece again.

"Now ten more times!" my father yelled.

I was exhausted. The demands of Balakirev's impossible composition had drained me. My fingers ached.

"No!" I told him.

"I'm telling you what to do, Lang Lang. Ten more times!"

"Forget it!" I screamed.

"Right now," my dad commanded. "Begin it again."

My friends looked at him, then at me, curious to watch the drama unfold.

"You are horrible!" I finally screamed in embarrassment, but perhaps given courage by my team of supporters.

"What did you call me?"

"Horrible! A crazy tyrant! A crazy storm trooper! A crazy cop! I am tired of your orders! Go to hell!"

My heart beat loudly as I said the words that I had wanted to say all my life. But now that they were said, now that I had humiliated my father in front of the other Chinese students, now that I had declared my independence, how would he react? Would he run to the piano and whack me across the mouth? Would he beat me on the head with a shoe? Would he curse me as I had cursed him?

He did none of those things.

Instead, he looked me in the eye with an expression I had never seen before, one of defeat and despair.

"I am leaving," he said. "I'm going back to China."

An hour later, he had packed his bag and caught a taxi for the airport. When my friends and I returned to the apartment and found him gone, I didn't know how to react. At first I was glad. Good riddance. This was what I wanted, wasn't it? To be free from my father? But if this was good, why was I so afraid? Why was remorse twisting my stomach? Why was I suddenly gripped with anxiety? Why did I, along with my Chinese friends, get into a cab and drive to the airport in hopes of convincing him to stay?

The truth was that I didn't want to be alone. I had lived with this man for so many years that the thought of *not* living with him was frightening.

We found him at the airport waiting on line to buy a ticket for China.

"This is crazy," I said. "Don't leave."

"You told me to go to hell. Right there, in front of your friends, you told me to go to hell."

"I'm sorry."

"Truly?"

"Truly."

"Then you want me to stay?"

"Yes, I want you to stay."

And he did, because that was all he needed to hear.

Cultural Tutor

Even once I became comfortable with English, I was still somewhat unsure about certain aspects of Western culture. My high school classes were shallow in their exploration of literature, art, and politics. If I was going to be a well-rounded artist, I knew I had to learn about more than music, and if I was to remain in my new adopted country, I wanted to understand it all on a deeper level.

One day at lunch at the Graffmans', I voiced my concern to Mrs. Graffman, a highly intelligent woman with vast cultural interests.

She was delighted by my curiosity and told me she had just the person for me to meet.

Richard Doran had been a professor of English at the University of Pennsylvania and was on the board at Curtis, the number two in the school's administration. Mrs. Graffman described him as an intellectual who was completely down-to-earth. An amateur piano player with a great interest in China, he had served as a city representative and as chief of staff to Pennsylvania's gov-

WITH THE DORANS AND MY DAD
AT THE HOLLYWOOD BOWL

ernor Milton Shapp back in the 1970s. He also loved sports. He sounded like the ideal cultural tutor for me.

"But would he be willing?" I asked.

"If I know Dick, he'll be eager."

It turned out she knew him quite well. Although Richard Doran was busy with a million activities, he took a personal interest in me and invited me to his home.

"I understand from Naomi Graffman," he said, "that you want me to give you piano lessons."

I smiled, unsure of whether I was understanding his English correctly, and said politely, "Yes, of course."

"Or maybe I misunderstood. Maybe she said you should give *me* lessons. The truth is, as far as my playing goes, I think I'm improving. After I played a little Schumann for Gary the other day, I asked him, 'What would Schumann think of my interpretation?' He said, 'The bad news is that I think it would give him a heart attack. But the good news is that the attack wouldn't be fatal.' It was the nicest compliment I'd gotten all day."

I liked this man immediately.

"Mr. Doran—" I started.

"Please call me Dick. I was once a professor. Now I'm just a civilian."

"Okay, Dick. I'm here because I need to know more about Western culture and the English language."

"A noble aim. And I can't deny that you've come to the right man. If it's the English language you want to know, the best place to start is Shakespeare."

"I'm ready," I said, up for any challenge.

"There's relatively easy Shakespeare, and then there's difficult Shakespeare. Which do you prefer?"

"Well, with music, I like tackling the most difficult piece first."

"Rachmaninoff? Tchaikovsky?" asked Dick.

"The harder the better," I said.

"Why do you like starting out that way?" he asked, amused.

"Once I can play the toughest composition, the rest seem easy."

"So it won't bother you to start our study of Shakespeare with *Hamlet*?" he asked.

"Not if you say it's the hardest."

"Yes, indeed," said Dick, using his favorite expression.

That very day we began. When Dick read the play to me, I didn't understand a thing.

"Hard enough?" he asked, knowing the answer.

"Yes, indeed!" I answered, imitating him good-naturedly, though I was starting to suspect I was in over my head.

He smiled and said, "We'll go slowly. We're going to study every line. I'll stop and explain the meaning, and I'll give you an idea of the meter. Iambic pentameter is one of the great meters in the history of all communication; Shakespeare used it for play after play. It is the basis of his poetry, his passion, and his meaning. Once you start feeling the meter, you'll start feeling Shakespeare."

Dick read for a while, then stopped to explain, and then he had me read. At first I was intimidated and tongue-tied, but his patience and encouragement kept me going. Within a few lessons, I was actually reading Shakespeare out loud and beginning to get a feel for his rhythms and characters. I loved the complexity of *Hamlet*, the way its themes overlap and the subtexts emerge like different melodies and counterpoints. Way before I fully understood the words, I could feel the shifts in moods and variations in tone—now light, now dark, now philosophical, now whimsical, all contained in the context of a gripping story of murder and the relationship between a son and his parents. Shakespeare's dialogue made me think of Mozart's phrasings, the way his music would change from personality to personality; through Shakespeare's characters and the way they interact with each other, I finally began to understand Mozart.

After a few weeks, when we had completed *Hamlet* and Dick was pleased with my grasp of the text, he announced that we would be going to a pop concert, which he claimed was an essential part of American culture.

The next thing I knew we were at *The Lion King* on Broadway, then back in Philly watching the 76ers play the Knicks, then off to a concert where, for the first time, I heard the great Luciano Pavarotti perform glorious arias by Puccini, Verdi, and Donizetti. Pavarotti instantly became one of my musical heroes.

Just when my head was filled with Italian opera, Dick said, "Now it's time for Gershwin."

The all-Gershwin concert we attended was a revelation. *Rhapsody in Blue* blew my mind, as did a performance of *Porgy and Bess*, whose melodies haunted my dreams for weeks. I was in awe of Gershwin's genius for infusing classical composition with African-American jazz.

"Now," said Dick, "we delve into politics. What do you know about the American political system?"

"Very little," I admitted.

"Not for long. Within a week, you'll know more than most Americans."

Dick was an expert. He was a lifelong Democrat, but he never imposed his views; he simply explained. He made sure I understood the difference between the Left and the Right in America, he gave me a tutorial on the history of the political parties, he walked me through the major events in the administrations of Eisenhower, Kennedy, Johnson, Nixon, Ford, Carter, Reagan, Bush, and Clinton. He whetted my interest in World War II, and I became a fanatic, reading anything I could get my hands on. Dick never ceased to surprise me with new pieces of information about history.

One day he said, "Nineteen eighty-two is perhaps the most important year of my life."

"Mine too," I said. "That's the year I was born."

"A fine coincidence. You see, in 1982 I directed Philly's tricentennial celebration. I arranged for the *Queen Elizabeth 2* to dock right here. Usually it docks in New York, but through my great powers of persuasion it arrived in the City of Brotherly Love. A delegation and I went aboard and sailed for China, where in Tianjin, the third-largest city in your marvelous country, I arranged a fellowship. Tianjin became a sister city of Philadelphia. Artisans from Tianjin came here and built Chinatown's Friendship Gate at Tenth and Arch streets. In my family, we refer to it as the Doran Memorial Gate. Have you seen it, Lang Lang?"

"I have."

"Do you love it?"

"Yes, indeed!"

Maestro Eschenbach

Early on I fell in love with American slang. Maybe because runaways and rebels formed the country, Americans applied the freedoms they found to their language as much as anything else. But also, ethnic groups from all over the world live here, and each has influenced American speech. American English is a mixture of everyone and everything. Perhaps that's why I finally eased my way into it. If I made a grammatical mistake, no one looked at me as if I had committed a crime. The language was loose; it seemed to let me off the hook when I went astray. It felt to me as if the language was there to be used—and played with—rather than honored.

For example, I heard classical musicians at Curtis talking about getting a gig.

"What's a gig?" I asked a friend.

"A short job," he said, "usually a one-night job."

"Where does the word come from?"

"Jazz musicians. They'll say, 'I got a gig last night playing at a nightclub.' Or they'll say, 'I was just hired to go on tour. I'm gigged-up for the rest of the year.'"

"And classical musicians don't mind using the same terms as jazz musicians?" I asked.

"Why should we? A gig's a gig."

"Gig." It felt good on my tongue.

Gigs were important. Getting good gigs was something my dad and I had been working toward for many years. Mr. Graffman had said that the good gigs would be forthcoming, that it was only a matter of time. Focus on the poetry of the music, not on the prizes. Avoid the contests; concentrate on the artistry. Be patient.

But patience was not easy for either me or my dad. After a year in Philadelphia, a year without seeing my mother, a year without a single trophy to add to my collection, a year without being called up to substitute in even a single concert, I grew restless. I wanted a gig.

When I brought up the problem with Mr. Graffman, he was understanding. "Concerts will come," he said. "But there's nothing you can do to speed up the process. When you're on the substitution list, you have no choice but to wait."

All my life, I had been in a hurry, and so had my dad. Suddenly we were told to stand still.

"Maybe there are some competitions out there that would be good to enter," my dad said one day.

"I think so," I agreed. "But how can we find out about them?"

My father suggested that I look through the classical music magazines, do some research. I went to the Curtis library one afternoon and found a number of periodicals that had long listings about upcoming contests. Sitting at a large table, I took out a yellow pad and carefully copied down the names of these competitions along with the entrance requirements. Just reading about the contests reignited the competitive spark in me.

"Hello, Lang Lang, nice to see you."

I looked up and was surprised to see Naomi Graffman.

"Hello, Mrs. Graffman. Nice to see you too."

She asked what I was working on so diligently, and I hesitated before answering. I knew her husband wouldn't approve. At the same time, I didn't want to lie.

"I'm researching piano competitions."

"You're thinking of entering some?"

I confessed that I was.

Mrs. Graffman expressed surprise. She knew about the conversation I'd had with her husband. She asked if I had changed my mind about following his advice.

"It isn't that I disagree with him," I told her. "It's just that I like winning."

"We all do, Lang Lang," she replied. "But sometimes it's important to understand the nature of true victory. If winning a contest keeps us from a bigger victory, then we haven't won at all, have we?"

I thought about what she said. "What's the bigger victory?" I asked.

"An international career that satisfies and sustains you for the rest of your life."

After considering the notion of a bigger victory, I tore up my list of competitions, and when I told Dad about my conversation with Mrs. Graffman, he said, "All right, Lang Lang. We'll go along with your teacher. But something has to happen. And soon."

It wasn't soon—at least not in my mind.

In my mind, I was the pianist who was going to combine the

sweetness of Rubinstein with the delicacy of Horowitz. For me, Rubinstein was the ultimate musician, while Horowitz was the ultimate pianist. To incorporate their greatness into a singular style that I could call my own—that was my dream. On certain days I was actually convinced that it was becoming a reality. Maybe it was the arrogance of youth, or maybe it was my competitive nature, which couldn't be held back for long. Whatever it was, it kept me asking the question: Where are the gigs?

Time passed. School progressed. My English improved. My practicing intensified. My lessons with Mr. Graffman put me in touch with a soulful poetry I applied to the piano. My heart yearned for my mother. We wrote and very occasionally she called. But those letters and calls only seemed to emphasize the great distance between us.

Now I was sixteen and I wanted more, but the paid engagements were few and far between. In the fall, I might find myself flying to a small city in New Mexico to play with an orchestra I had never heard of. The audience might be appreciative, but the orchestra would be full of perfectly nice musicians who unfortunately played out of tune. And the pay would be paltry. In the spring, my father and I might drive to an even smaller city somewhere in Pennsylvania where the concert hall would be half-full and the audience indifferent. This wasn't the American dream I had envisioned.

"Don't worry," the management firm said. "There are some big orchestras that want to employ you."

"Which ones?" I asked.

"Knoxville."

"Where is that?" I wondered.

"In Tennessee. A fine orchestra."

But eventually, the Knoxville Symphony Orchestra turned me down. So did the Milwaukee.

"He's too young," they said. "Too inexperienced. Too unknown."

"There will be more opportunities," management kept promising. "Houston is interested."

Houston came through, but it was an outdoor venue, and in the summertime Houston is hotter than hell. They had an air conditioner blowing onstage that cooled my left hand, but my right hand was sweating like crazy. The keys were wet with humidity. In the front rows, babies were crying.

Dad grew restless. He went to the grocery store, bought his vegetables, cooked our meals, and wandered around Curtis futilely eavesdropping on private lessons and going to lectures, making sure I was up on the latest developments. He monitored my practice and kept asking whether I'd heard from the management company.

"You have anything lined up for me?" I asked management. "Anything at all?"

"We're getting resistance."

"Why?" I asked.

"They think a sixteen-year-old kid can't understand Brahms or Liszt."

"They're wrong," I said.

"We tell them that. We tell them to look at your videotapes and to listen to your discs. But people are stubborn."

"I want to work."

"We want you to as well. When you make money, we make money. We'll get back to you."

"What did they say?" my father asked when I hung up the phone.

"They said I have to be patient."

"You need to push them," he said.

"I just did."

"Push them harder."

"How hard can we push?"

"Very hard," my father insisted.

I understood Dad's tenacity. In China, he could take the bull by the horns and push as hard as he wanted to, but because he still hadn't learned English, he was forced to push me to push them, and I was just a kid.

Meanwhile, it was practice, practice, practice; I was preparing orchestral pieces, but I couldn't help but wonder whether those pieces would ever be performed.

Fall, winter, spring.

No calls, no gigs. But I was still practicing eight hours a day.

The summer of 1998 was brutally hot.

Then, in September, a break. Finally. The Baltimore Symphony Orchestra and its director, David Zinman, were world renowned. They had toured Europe and Asia many times. They had won Grammys with records that they had made with Yo-Yo Ma. The Baltimore Symphony was big-time. And they wanted me to play with them. But after Baltimore, my life didn't change. I was still waiting for a bigger opportunity to wake America up.

"Ten years?" I asked management.

"Yes, ten years at least."

We were talking about the possibility of playing with the great Chicago Symphony Orchestra. I had just played Beethoven's Choral Fantasy in Baltimore, and the reviews had been so positive I was certain I'd get a shot at performing with one of the Big Five American orchestras. Because of its stellar brass section and brilliant conductor, Daniel Barenboim, I saw Chicago as the perfect place to begin. But my management told me that ten years would be the normal wait to play with an orchestra of that caliber.

"Did you tell them that you're not a normal boy?" my dad asked me when I told him about the conversation. "Did you tell them about your great success in Baltimore?"

"They have the reviews, Dad. They know everything."

"Then why aren't they doing more?" he asked.

I wondered the same thing.

Cleveland has a great orchestra, and when the resident conductor, an Indonesian named Jahja Ling, asked me to audition for it at Carnegie Hall while it was in New York, my dad and I ran up to the city. I performed well and felt confident that Cleveland would soon be calling me. In my happy state, I looked forward to the train ride back to Philadelphia, where, after the grueling audition, I could sit back and relax.

"We're not taking the train," said Dad, "we're taking the bus. It's cheaper."

I thought my father meant that we would head over to the Port Authority to take the Greyhound, but instead he led me to Chinatown, where he had learned that you could ride to Philadelphia for only five dollars. The bumpy ride on the broken-down, overcrowded bus dampened my spirits, but I remained optimistic, sure that I'd soon be invited to Cleveland and debut with one of the Big Five American orchestras.

But time passed slowly. The phone rang infrequently, and when it did, management was not calling about exciting gigs. Cleveland still had not fixed a date for me.

It was 1999, my seventeenth birthday had come and gone, and the summer seemed long and hot. Dad and I were restless. We wanted action, gigs, recognition, and good fees. In the warm evenings, I'd leave the apartment after practicing and wander down to the big Barnes & Noble bookstore to look through classical music magazines. One night, my father came with me. We leafed through *Gramophone* and *BBC Music Magazine*. Both featured detailed articles about the upcoming Gala of the Century at Ravinia, summer home of the Chicago Symphony Orchestra. Ravinia is the oldest outdoor venue in North America, where everyone from Pablo Casals to George Gershwin has performed. The musical director, Christoph Eschenbach, and the executive director, Zarin Mehta, were organizing the August gala that would headline the violinists Isaac Stern and Midori, in addition to the pianists André Watts, Leon Fleisher, and Alicia de Larrocha.

"This is where you should be playing," said my father.

"I agree."

"Tell management."

But telling management never seemed to get me anywhere. I didn't even bother to buy the magazines. Reading about the upcoming Ravinia gala would only frustrate me more. Instead, we went home and ate leftover chicken.

That night the phone rang.

"You don't know me," said a woman at the other end, "but I work for Ravinia, the outdoor music festival. Have you heard of it?"

"Yes, I have," I said, amazed at the coincidence.

"Well, I happened to be in Carnegie Hall the day you auditioned for the Cleveland Orchestra, and I must say I was impressed. I mentioned you to Maestro Eschenbach, who said he'd be happy to give you a twenty-minute audition if you'd come to Ravinia. Of course he's terribly busy, but if he likes the way you play, there's a possibility of booking you sometime this coming fall or winter. Are you willing?"

Was I willing? I was thrilled. The next thing I knew, my dad and I were flying high over Lake Michigan. In the distance I saw the Sears Tower and the John Hancock Center. As we soared above the bright beauty of Chicago's skyscrapers, I was exhilarated. I felt that fate had had a hand in bringing me to Ravinia; my hopes had lain low for so long, and now they felt out of control.

When we landed, we took a taxi to Highland Park, the suburb that houses Ravinia. The audition was held not on the outdoor stage but in the smaller recital hall, Martin Theatre. When I arrived, I was starving, so I grabbed a turkey sandwich from the kitchen, wolfed it down, and started warming up on the stage. When I looked up, a man stood over me. He looked exactly like Yul Brynner in *The King and I*. He was completely bald, and his stance—legs slightly apart, arms folded over his waist—looked threatening. I recognized him as Maestro Christoph Eschenbach.

"Maestro," I said, getting to my feet. "I just want to say how much I admire you, both as a conductor and as a pianist." I was tripping over the words. How does one talk to a man such as Christoph Eschenbach?

"Thank you. What do you have for me today?"

I was ready. I had been preparing for this moment for years. My heart pounded inside my chest, not with fear but with anticipation and joy.

"I have a Haydn," I said. "I have a Brahms. I have a Rachmaninoff. I have a Mozart."

"Let's start with the traditional," said Maestro. "Let's start with Haydn."

I played a Haydn E major sonata. I felt as though I played it flawlessly.

"Fine," Maestro commented. "Now Brahms."

"I have the intermezzi. It will take another twenty minutes. Do you have time, Maestro?"

"Yes, I have time. I want to hear your Brahms."

The Brahms went well.

"What else?" asked Maestro.

"Rachmaninoff Sonata no. 2."

"Ah, the romantic one. Please play it."

I played it with every romantic impulse in my body. By then the twenty-minute audition had gone on for an hour.

"Do you have Scriabin?" he asked.

"Yes," I said. "I have his études."

"Excellent. Proceed."

I danced through the études.

"You mentioned Mozart. You have Mozart?"

"Yes, Maestro. I have a great deal of Mozart."

I played a great deal of Mozart.

"Beethoven?" asked the conductor.

"What Beethoven would you like to hear, Maestro?"

He named some sonatas. I played them all.

"My God!" said Maestro when I was through. "I've lost track of the time. I've been here nearly two hours and missed my rehearsal!" He asked if I could sit for another minute—he would be right back with their executive director. Maestro returned with Mr. Mehta, who asked to hear Schumann. Then Chopin, then Liszt.

"How many concertos do you have?" asked Mr. Mehta.

"I have thirty. I have twenty of those completely memorized."

"Which ones?" asked Maestro.

I rattled off the names of the big ones—Tchaikovsky, Rachmaninoff, Prokofiev, Beethoven.

"If you had a choice, which would you play as your debut with the Chicago Symphony?"

The very thought thrilled me. I almost said Rachmaninoff no. 3, but at the last second I said Tchaikovsky no. 1, because I remembered how many careers were galvanized by that piece—Horowitz's, Rubinstein's, Richter's.

"Fine," said Mr. Mehta. "I must go now, and Maestro is also late for an engagement. But we thank you for your time, and you will be hearing from us shortly." We shook hands, and that was it.

I was elated. I had played for nearly three hours. I had played more than an audition; I had played a private recital. On the plane back to Philly, my father said, "By fall, you will be concertizing in Chicago. You will be playing with one of the Big Five."

"I hope I can wait until then," I said.

"You have no choice," said Dad.

That night my dreams were wild. I was sailing over Lake Michigan and flying over downtown Chicago. My piano was my airplane, first a prop plane, then a small jet, then a jumbo jet, then a rocket ship orbiting the globe. The ringing phone woke me up. I looked at the clock and saw it said 8:00 a.m. Management was on the line.

"Please call me later," I said. "It's too early. I can't even think."

"When you hear what I have to say, you'll understand why that's not possible."

I yawned and half listened.

"André Watts is due to play Ravinia tonight, but he's too sick to go on. He has a fever. They need a replacement. They want you."

I was convinced this was part of my dream. I was back on the rocket ship zooming around the globe.

"Lang Lang," said management, "are you there? You're to play with the Chicago Symphony. Tonight. They want the first movement of Tchaikovsky no. 1. You need to be at the airport in ninety minutes. You need to get up and get going. *Now!*"

I jumped out of bed. I woke up my dad, told him the news, started jumping up and down.

"You misunderstood," he said. "Your English failed you, and you misunderstood."

"I understood every single word, Dad. Get dressed. A car will pick us up in twenty minutes."

For the next twenty-four hours—surely the most surreal twenty-four hours of my life—I found myself walking through a different kind of dream, a waking dream, the dream I had been designing since I was a boy back in Shenyang. It began when my dad and I got on the plane back to Chicago. On the flight, I played the Tchaikovsky, my hands running over an invisible keyboard in midair. I heard the mighty Chicago brass in my ears; I saw the expanse of thirty thousand fans seated before me. I was daydreaming and loving every minute of it.

At the airport, instead of taking a taxi as we had done the previous day, we sat in the back of a long Lincoln Town Car in which a uniformed driver, who said, "Hello, Mr. Lang, welcome to Chicago," whisked us to Ravinia for rehearsals. Maestro was waiting for me. Next to him was Isaac Stern, the same Isaac Stern who, in his famous video *From Mao to Mozart*, had toured China and won the hearts of my countrymen. Next to Stern was Leon Fleisher, the great American pianist and dear friend of Mr. Graffman's. Next to Fleisher was Alicia de Larrocha, the most famous pianist in Spain and one of the best in the world, a woman I had long admired.

"We've heard so much about you, Lang Lang," she said. "We came to hear your rehearsal."

I was too flabbergasted to respond. All I could do was smile and bow.

And so the dream continued. It was the first time I had ever played Tchaikovsky with a great orchestra. Maestro looked at me in amazement and said, "It is as though we have been rehearsing this concerto together for weeks." I felt the same way. I was floating on air. Only a few days earlier I was reading about the Gala of the Century in a magazine, imagining the thrill of playing with the Chicago Symphony Orchestra but having been told that joy was at least ten years off. Now that joy was mine. Now I was in the dressing room putting on my tailless tux and, with the door half-open, listening to the pianists perform before me: the fabulous Leon Fleisher playing the Brahms First, the magnificent de Larrocha playing Granados's *Goyescas*. I peeked out and saw that inside the tent people were swarming—five thousand I had been told. On the lawn and on the hill were another twenty-five thousand. The weather was perfect, not too humid, not too hot, a gentle breeze, a luminous moon.

My time had come.

The crowd was expecting André Watts, but Isaac Stern came to the stage instead to announce the news that I was to replace Watts. He did so with singular charm and grace. He explained Watts's absence but promised the audience that they wouldn't forget what they were about to hear. He talked about this newcomer from China who was only seventeen years old. He spoke of me with warmth and enthusiasm, and by the time Maestro Eschenbach and I walked onstage, the crowd, as well as the international press, was brimming with curiosity.

I thought of Michael Jordan and Tiger Woods, and in my mind I transformed their most brilliant moves into my playing: I imagined Jordan's slam dunk as the big beginning of the Tchaikovsky chords; I thought of Tiger Woods's swing while playing the octaves. The Chicago Symphony's brass section was the most powerful sound I had ever heard in my life, and thanks to the orchestra I played better than I had ever played before. I knew that this dream was no dream, it was real; my chance had come, and I couldn't afford to be anything but my absolute best. Maestro, the great orchestra, and I became one. I felt myself floating outside myself, over a body of music effortlessly moving through me and directing my fingers to do things they had never done before.

When I struck the last note, there was a silence, then an explosion. A jolt. "An electrical charge," one of the critics called it. And suddenly thirty thousand people leaped to their feet. From the stage, it felt to me as if all thirty thousand people were shouting "Bravo! Bravo! Bravo!" It was the moment of a lifetime. In my heart, I knew it was the beginning of something new, the beginning of a new life.

After the concert, a dinner was held for invited guests in a huge tent on the lawn. I was still flying high, receiving compliment after compliment, being treated like a star. At our table, Isaac Stern toasted me on what he called "the launch of a long and brilliant career." Midori, a prodigy violinist from Japan who had been a childhood idol of mine, sat next to me, making sure I ate my vegetables and fish. Maestro Eschenbach and Mr. Mehta raised glasses in my honor. I drank orange juice in place of champagne—I've never liked liquor or wine—but I certainly was high on this unrestrained adulation.

"Lang Lang," said Mr. Mehta, "when we asked you to substitute for André tonight, we knew you'd play well. But we never expected a success on so grand a scale. This is one of the greatest evenings in the history of Ravinia. It will be remembered for decades to come. In fact, so great is this evening that I don't want it to end. Maestro and I have been talking and we're wondering if you'd play something else."

"Tonight?" I asked.

"Yes, tonight," said Maestro. "We'd love to hear you play the *Goldberg Variations*."

"I don't have the score," I said.

"Surely you have it memorized," said Mr. Mehta.

"But where will I play it?"

"We'll open up the Martin Theatre, and you'll give us a private recital."

It was nearly 2:00 a.m. Everyone but the featured artists had gone home, and they wanted to stay and hear me play.

I had learned Bach's *Goldberg Variations* when I moved to the United States over two years earlier, and I had not played it very often. The composition was an hour and twenty minutes long. At one time I had it all in my head, but did I still know it? I was doubtful. It was then that I realized what Mr. Mehta and Maestro had in mind. They wanted to underscore the historic importance of the evening. When André Watts was sixteen, he had replaced Glenn Gould, whose signature piece was the *Goldberg Variations*. Now they wanted to connect the dots between Gould, Watts, and me.

"Are you sure you know it?" my father whispered in my ear when I translated the request to him.

"No, I'm not sure," I admitted.

"What will you do?" he asked.

"I have no choice," I said. "When Christoph Eschenbach and Zarin Mehta make a request, I cannot say no."

The next thing I knew, we were being driven in a golf cart over to the Martin, where I had auditioned for Maestro just the day before. Maestro acted as my stage manager, turning on the lights, finding a piano stool, adjusting its height, and making sure I was comfortable. Then he, along with the distinguished artists who had come along, sat in the front row.

Before I began, my dad patted me on the back and said, "Don't worry, you will remember every single note." And I did. Bach's *Goldberg Variations* came back to me as though I were in a dream, the same waking dream that had begun when the phone had rung some eighteen hours earlier, rousing me from sleep. The legend of the *Variations* was that Bach had written it for his friend Johann Gottlieb Goldberg because Goldberg could not sleep. As an inducement to sleep, the *Goldberg Variations* is a failure, but as a work of music it is a masterpiece and one of the most difficult pieces to play. It was the final act of the most astounding day of my life.

It was 6:00 a.m. before I was able to fall asleep in my hotel suite. Day was breaking; I was exhausted, but my mind couldn't stop reeling. Sleep finally came, but when it did, I was still hearing a strange combination of Tchaikovsky's First and Bach's *Goldberg Variations.*

The Big Five

They all came calling.

Chicago was first, paving the way, but then the other four great American orchestras—New York, Boston, Philadelphia, and Cleveland—extended invitations.

The news about Ravinia had quickly circulated around the classical music world: a teenager had replaced André Watts and set the festival on fire. The kid was amazing, he could play virtually every piano concerto ever written. He was a crowd-pleaser, a dramatic performer who loved nothing more than to convey his love of the music. The *Chicago Tribune* called me the biggest, most exciting keyboard talent encountered in many years.

"I heard it was a lovefest in Ravinia," said Mr. Graffman a week later, when we were back in Philly.

"I loved it—that's for sure," I said. While I was playing Ravinia, Mr. Graffman had been in China. He had missed the concert but had received firsthand reports from Leon Fleisher and Isaac Stern.

I apologized to my teacher for doubting his plan. If I had entered a contest against his will, I would probably have been off competing in some European country rather than on the verge of a real career.

Mr. Graffman laughed. "You're young and eager, Lang Lang. You have powerful motivation—and that's a wonderful trait. You're in the spotlight, and I'm certain you'll remain there for the rest of your life." But he warned me that while the spotlight brought the kind of attention I'd long sought, it could also bring the kind of attention I hadn't considered—the fickle opinions of the critics. "At the moment you've got a couple of good reviews. You're the new golden boy. But no one remains the golden boy for long. New artists who burst onto the scene and win the hearts of the public are usually given a honeymoon. It might last a year or two. Then the critics start sharpening their knives. It doesn't happen in every case, but often enough to be forewarned. Still, no matter how the press views you, you'll be fine—as long as you have the respect of your fellow musicians and the love of the public."

I thanked Mr. Graffman for his advice, but once again I wasn't completely sure he was right. After all, I hadn't received a negative notice yet. Why should that change? Practically every day a new offer came in from a different orchestra, and now I had my choice of two recording contracts, one from Deutsche Grammophon and one from Telarc. I chose Telarc, even though it was a lesser-known label, because of the personal attention I was promised.

My first release was a live performance in Seiji Ozawa Hall at Tanglewood. It was a recording of a recital that included Haydn, Rachmaninoff, Brahms, Tchaikovsky, and Balakirev. The cover photograph on the CD shows an eighteen-year-old boy, slightly chubby, slightly nerdy, dressed in a tux. Someone said, "Lang Lang, you look like a manchild."

I didn't mind. I just wanted to perform. I was so thrilled at having finally broken through the barriers to a professional career that I was practically giddy when management presented me with a list of upcoming engagements: a European debut with Maestro Yuri Temirkanov and the St. Petersburg Philharmonic Orchestra of Russia, a London debut at the Proms playing Rachmaninoff's Third Piano Concerto, a Carnegie

Hall debut with Temirkanov and the Baltimore Symphony Orchestra, not to mention concerts with the symphonies of San Francisco, St. Louis, Dallas, Phoenix, and Vancouver and recitals in Munich, Zurich, Los Angeles, Seattle, and Lincoln Center in New York City.

Emotionally, I didn't cope with all this very well.

Of course I was grateful, but because it all happened so quickly, my head didn't have a chance to catch up with my heart. Part of the problem was this: I had gone from playing twenty little gigs a year to playing practically eighty; it was like a soccer team going from Series D to Series A in one season. The whirlwind schedule had left me unsettled; it felt as if my head were in one place and my body in another. I was still a student at Curtis, after all, with homework assignments to complete; I was constantly calling friends from the road to catch up on lessons I had missed. Plane travel was hectic and sometimes a little frightening. There was the pressure of schedules and visa renewals. There were thunderstorms and lightning, turbulence in the air and passport trouble on the ground. My piano lessons with Mr. Graffman were conducted over the telephone, which was a challenge to say the least. Just when I got settled into a city, my father was there to remind me that we were due at the airport at 6:30 a.m. sharp.

I was slow in adjusting to the rhythms of success. In my new public role, I was meeting interesting new people every day. If, for example, in Los Angeles I met a girl I liked, I'd barely get to know her before it was time to leave. The same thing was true with new friends. I make friends easily, they make life worthwhile for me, but who can sustain a friendship when, after a day or two, you say goodbye and perhaps won't see each other for a year?

I had finally started earning good money. When my grandfather called from China and asked how much I was getting for each performance, I answered, "Five." "Five hundred?" he asked, incredulous. When I said no, he asked, "Fifty?" When I told him I was receiving five thousand dollars per concert, he was stunned. I bought a house in downtown Philly, yet I never stayed for long; I was always on the road. People said, "Lang Lang, why do you need a big house? Just rent an apartment in a high-rise." Yet owning a home was, for me, an important part of my American dream. In China, we had never been able to own a home.

Best of all I finally got to see my mom. When I first began earning money and we could afford to call her in Shenyang, that felt like the greatest luxury. Now buying a ticket for her travel was no longer a problem. But because she could not get a green card, she could only stay with me a short while. And because I had already begun to run from city to city playing concert after concert—a pattern that continues to this day—our time together was always truncated. We never had as much as an entire week or two when we could simply be alone and visit.

Nonetheless, to have Mom in Philadelphia was a great joy. I had not seen her for practically three years. The first time she walked through customs at the airport, I started to cry like a little boy, and when she held me in her arms, I felt like one. For the next two days, until we all flew to a faraway concert, I didn't let her out of my sight. We spoke late into the night.

"Is success everything you dreamed it would be, Lang Lang?" she asked.

I told her about the difficulties I was having adjusting to the breakneck schedule, of leaving new friends I had just made, and about the problems that came with nonstop travel. I also talked about feeling a deeper love for music than I ever had before. I told her things I had never confessed to anyone—that when I practiced, I chanted for what I wanted. Over and over again, I would chant, "Get me a Carnegie Hall recital, get me a Carnegie Hall recital, get me a big homecoming tour in China, get me a big homecoming tour in China." My mother assured me that I would return to China soon. "Everyone remembers you," she told me. "China wants Lang Lang." It turned out, though, that she wasn't quite right.

PART FIVE

CITIZEN OF

THE WORLD

Homecoming

We are all, of course, born of our beloved mothers; my own mother is the single most important source of my sanity—my love for her is boundless. But we also have metaphorical mothers. China, where all rivers are regarded in maternal terms, is the country that mothered me.

Yet because the cultural ties between Russia and China are strongest when it comes to music, Russia also nourished me in many ways. Early on, I was told that I have a Russian soul. Somehow I feel that Russian music is in my blood.

As both a child and a teenager, I viewed Russian compositions as the ultimate musical constructions. Their complexity challenged and dazzled me on the deepest levels, both emotionally and intellectually. My career had taken off in Ravinia playing the work of Tchaikovsky. So it was a thrill, in December 2000, at the age of eighteen, to find myself walking the streets of St. Petersburg, looking at the amazing configuration of ancient churches and glorious buildings. The next day I was to make my Eastern European debut in the city that was Russia's cultural heart, and as I walked, I could hear in my head Rachmaninoff's Second Piano Concerto, the piece that I'd be playing with the St. Petersburg Philharmonic Orchestra. I'd performed it before, but never here in the country of its birth, and never before an audience of Russian cognoscenti.

Adding to the thrill was the fact that I'd be performing back-to-back concerts with Evgeny Kissin, a Russian pianist ten years my senior whom I had loved since I was a young boy. Kissin occupied the practice room next to mine, and I was excited to be in such close proximity to a man I admired so deeply.

I took the stage with Horowitz on my mind, Horowitz whose triumphant homecoming concert in Russia in 1986 after a sixty-year absence had been caught on a film that I had watched countless times. I bowed before an audience that I knew was probably the most discriminating I had ever faced, seated myself at the piano, and proceeded to interpret one of their greatest composers' greatest compositions. After the Rachmaninoff 3, I played his second sonata as well as Tchaikovsky, Scriabin, and Balakirev's formidable *Islamey*, the piece that had almost ruptured the relationship between me and my father back in Philly.

It was an all-Russian program on Russian soil before Russian lovers of Russian music. How would they react to a Chinese kid taking on their most cherished repertoire? They stood and cheered for six long minutes, among the happiest minutes of my life.

The next day the Russian press reported that in the twentieth century a pianist from Texas, Van Cliburn, had shaken up the world of classical music by coming to Moscow and winning the International Tchaikovsky Competition. Now, the writer continued, on the eve of the new millennium, a Chinese teenager had arrived to take the country by storm. Thank you, Mother Russia.

■

The word came back definitively.

"Sorry," said management, "but the Chinese presenters are saying that Lang Lang is no longer a big deal in China. They say that there are a number of other young pianists with bigger reputations—pianists who are recent winners of major competitions. When they asked us to name recent contests you have won, we explained that you are above that sort of thing. That didn't go over well with the Chinese. They said they need winners."

The story was this: I'd been looking for a big moment to return to China, and I was convinced that moment would be with the New York Philharmonic. Zarin Mehta had been appointed executive director and Maestro Loren Maazel music director. They wanted me to play their first concert in New York and then tour Asia with the orchestra, including stops in Beijing and Shanghai. Naturally I was thrilled.

But a week later, the Philadelphia Orchestra called and said 2001 would be Maestro Wolfgang Sawallisch's last Asian tour before his retirement. The year would also mark the orchestra's hundredth anniversary. They wanted me to play a grand concert with them in the Great Hall of the People in Beijing. The president would be in attendance, and the whole country would be watching. Even better, the event was scheduled before the New York Philharmonic tour, so I could do both.

Now I was ecstatic. I'd be returning home with the same orchestra that had accompanied Nixon!

But of course this new development complicated matters: New York requested that I play something other than the Rachmaninoff Piano Concerto no. 2 with Philly, since I was planning to play that piece with the New York Philharmonic. I offered to play a Mendelssohn concerto.

Fortunately, Philly was gracious enough to understand.

But the situation was far from perfect. The Chinese presenters weren't happy. "When Philadelphia plays in the Great Hall of the People," they said, "we want them to come with a huge international star. Lang Lang is hardly a world-renowned name. In China, Lang Lang is all but forgotten." They told the Philadelphia Orchestra that I was unacceptable as a featured soloist.

Philly was surprised—they had thought that the presenters would be thrilled to have me. "Big star, we need a big star," they kept insisting.

I was heartbroken. I had envisioned my return to China as the most glorious moment of my life. China was home. China was where I had learned to love piano. China had given me the foundation that had allowed me to grow as an artist, had admitted me to its most prestigious music conservatory, had celebrated my many victories as a child. How could China reject me now?

Maestro Sawallisch told me that the Chinese presenters were adamant. He told me that the orchestra would confer and get back to me. Days passed. I despaired, convinced that my homecoming with the Philadelphia Orchestra wasn't going to happen.

The phone finally rang.

"We've been in touch with the Chinese presenters," said Maestro Sawallisch. "They're still not budging. They mentioned the name of a Chinese pianist who had just won an important competition, but I refused. I'd never heard of this player. Then they offered another concert pianist who was the most recent winner of another competition, but I hadn't heard of this person either, so I refused again. 'Look, gentlemen,' I finally said, 'it comes down to this. We want Lang Lang because Lang Lang is not only part of China but part of Philadelphia. We have a letter from the governor of Pennsylvania supporting Lang Lang in which he calls him "our adopted Philadelphian." He's a proud student of Curtis, a brilliant pianist, and the one artist we feel is most suited to be featured on our tour.' We said, 'If you don't want Lang Lang, we refuse to come to China.' "

I was stunned. "How did they respond to that?" I asked.

"They didn't. They said they'd think it over."

"And if they say no?" I asked.

"Then it's no go. No Lang Lang, no Philadelphia Orchestra concert."

I was overwhelmed by the degree of their support. When I told my father, he said that the Chinese presenters would have to concede, that the prestige of having the Philadelphia Orchestra in the Great Hall of the People was too great to pass up. But I wasn't as sure.

More days passed, more waiting, more worrying.

Then the call.

"The Chinese presenters have agreed. The concert is on."

But only a few weeks later, it looked like the concert was off.

U.S. relations with China were fraught. Because of various incidents that took place during that period, tensions were high, leading the Boston Symphony Orchestra to cancel its tour of China. In the spring of 2001, a U.S. spy plane collided with one of two Chinese jet fighter planes, and a Chinese pilot, Wang Wei, was killed. The United States claimed it was flying over "international airspace," but China said the incident happened over Chinese "air territory."

For many days, our touring plans were put on hold until the diplomats sorted out the situation. The controversy seemed to build, and I became more distraught. I wanted to go home, I wanted to see my mom, I wanted to play in the Great Hall of the People with the great Philadelphia Orchestra; I worried that the concerts would be canceled as they had been in 1999. Beyond my professional ambitions, though, the fact that the two countries I loved so much could be at such odds pained me.

More days of suspense. More nerve-racking phone calls. More uncertainty.

Then the call.

"It's on," a U.S. official informed us. "You and Philadelphia are free to go."

The glitch was that my father couldn't go with us. If he left the United States, he might not get a U.S. visa to return. The United States was now our headquarters, and he needed to be there when I returned. Meanwhile, between now and then, I had an important date to play: my debut concert at Carnegie Hall.

It took place on April 26, 2001, and I was especially pleased to be performing my debut with the Baltimore Symphony Orchestra under Maestro Yuri Temirkanov. I loved the Baltimore Symphony because it was the first major American orchestra to give me a break, and of course I had loved Carnegie Hall even before I saw it for myself during that first trip to New York when I played at Steinway Hall. To play Carnegie Hall was to be in the living presence of Horowitz and Rubinstein, my masters who had performed there countless times. It had by far the best acoustics I'd ever experienced; between the inspirational setting, where I could feel the presence, and love for music, of all the performers who had played before me, and the spectacular sound, I felt I was flying through the sky, diving deep into water. For the first time in my life, as I played, the piano and I became one.

I played the Grieg Piano Concerto in A Minor, op. 16. Some consider it a corny piece, but I love it and tried to convey its bold lyricism. I was cheered by the audience and lauded by the critics. One writer said that I expressed freedom with tempo and dynamic changes—brave of an eighteen-year-old who still hadn't completed his studies at Curtis.

After the triumph at Carnegie Hall, I was ready to go home. For all the politics surrounding my date at the Great Hall of the People with the Philadelphia Orchestra, my attitude hadn't changed: this was the homecoming I had dreamed of.

In the four years that I had been away from home, I had become a different person, a different artist. I had arrived in the United States still a child, obedient to the demands and discipline of my father; I was now on the brink of adulthood, a young man who made my own decisions and translated this new world for my father, who was still rooted in the old. Since leaving China, I had spent four years practicing the piano six, seven, or eight hours every single day. I had grown as a musician under the tutelage of Gary Graffman, who had changed my outlook, even my very sense of identity.

I wanted China, my beloved motherland, to be proud of me. I wanted China to see who I had become and welcome me with open arms.

The Press

My first press conference took place in Beijing only a day after I had flown in from Philly. It was the end of May 2001, and my mother was by my side. Back in America, my father was calling every half hour to find out what was happening.

I stood at a podium as Chinese reporters shouted questions at me. Cameras were rolling.

"What have you been doing since you left China?" asked one reporter.

"Practicing," I said.

Everyone laughed. Then I spoke about substituting for André Watts at Ravinia and my Carnegie Hall debut.

"What contests have you won?" asked another reporter.

IN THE FORBIDDEN CITY,
DRESSED AS AN EMPEROR
FROM THE QING DYNASTY

I explained that the American system was different. After a certain point, you weren't expected to compete.

"If you haven't won any awards," said a third reporter, "why did Philadelphia choose you?"

"I guess because they like me," I replied.

No one laughed. Everyone wanted to hear about the competitions, and when my explanations didn't suit them, their questioning became hostile.

"Do you think you could triumph in today's major contests?"

"Would you be willing to enter competitions while you're back here in China?"

"How can we know how you measure up if you have no awards to show for yourself?"

The press conference was so brutal that even the joy of being reunited with my mother had faded.

"They will all change their tune once they hear you play," she told me afterward.

My father was furious. "If I were there," he said, "I'd tell them all to go straight to hell."

For that reason, I'm glad he wasn't there.

Maestro Sawallisch couldn't have been more supportive. He took up my part and told the reporters that I was a wonderful piano player and that competition was not a measurement of the quality of play. But the reporters paid little attention.

When I gave individual interviews later that day, their skepticism about my four years in America was still evident. I explained the different paradigm in the United States, the different approach to launching a career—but my explanation fell on deaf ears.

I was sick of arguing and justifying myself.

"What's the point?" asked Maestro Sawallisch. "All questions will be answered when you play at the Great Hall of the People."

The concert went well. My mother and many relatives from Shenyang were there, and though the Great Hall of the People is not a concert hall but a conference hall that holds ten thousand seats and we needed to use a microphone because of the bad acoustics, it was a tremendous joy to perform in the hall that is the seat of Chinese political power. But Mendelssohn is not Rachmaninoff. Mendelssohn is beautiful, lyrical, sensitive, even glorious. The Chinese public wasn't waiting for sensitive and beautiful. They wanted a high-tech piece that would justify my lack of prizes over the past four years. They wanted to be knocked over. They were certainly pleased, and they were certainly kind, but I knew they had expected more. I didn't explain that I was playing a relatively modest piece in deference to my upcoming Chinese tour with the New York Philharmonic, because I didn't want to disparage Philadelphia. At the Great Hall, my encore was "Liu Yang River," which I dedicated to Professor Zhu and Professor Zhao, "my two beloved teachers, without whom I would not be playing for you today."

I was received with warm applause.

"How long did they applaud?" my father asked. He was calling from Philly.

"A long time."

"Were there cheers and bravos? Did you get a standing ovation?"

"Come on, Dad. You've been in America too long. You forget that in China we applaud. We do not stand and cheer."

"I thought they would have cheered you."

"They were nice."

"And the press?"

"I think they're getting there."

"Eventually the Chinese press will love you. It'll take time, though. They don't like the idea that your career is being built in America, not in China."

Three months later, in August 2001, I made my Western European debut, at the BBC Proms in the Royal Albert Hall in London, playing the same repertoire I had performed in St. Petersburg, Rachmaninoff's Third Piano Concerto with Maestro Yuri Temirkanov conducting the St. Petersburg Philharmonic Orchestra. The capacity audience showered me with affection, as did the critics. *The London Times* wrote, "This could well be history in the making." It was a thrilling experience, and I dreamed that China would one day embrace me with equal enthusiasm.

The Critics

As the plane crossed the Pacific and then the great mainland of America, my head started aching and my mind turned fuzzy. I was reading Hemingway's *Old Man and the Sea*, a story I loved; Hemingway's language was simple, emotional, and easy for me to understand. He wrote with his heart, not with his head. And yet I was having a hard time comprehending his words. By the time I cleared customs, I was sick. My dad rushed me home, where I slept for a week, chilled and feverish. At the first indications that I was recovering, my father chided me for having missed too much practice.

I had graduated Curtis in May 2002; it was nearly July 2002, and I was returning to Ravinia for five days with Maestro Eschenbach. They were calling my stay there the Lang Lang residency, and I would be playing five different concerts all with difficult programs, including the Rachmaninoff Paganini Variations, the Grieg, and a chamber music concert. Ravinia had taken me to the next level and had brought me a prominence that had made these last two whirlwind years possible, and I couldn't wait to return. In the last twenty-four months, I had become the golden boy, and now, with this third visit to Ravinia, I'd return in triumph to the place where my new life had begun.

How can a critic tell me what Tchaikovsky had in mind when that critic has never met Tchaikovsky? How can anyone know how Rachmaninoff intended a piece to be played? We are all interpreting a text. There are no literal instructions, for example, for how hard to press the keys or how emotionally or unemotionally to employ rubato. Playing music is not rocket science. It is poetry, romance. Musically, how do you convey longing? Anger? Fear? Jubilation? Confusion? Clarity? You look at the text, you look inside yourself, and you come up with an interpretation. Yes, that interpretation is born out of something that has been written by someone you don't know; but your interpretation must be the genuine manifestation of something you do know: human emotion.

At Ravinia, I was eviscerated by the same critic who had raved about my performance there three years earlier. I had never experienced anything like it. He wrote that I ruined Tchaikovsky and massacred Rachmaninoff. He hated the performance and blamed Maestro for shamelessly supporting a crazy pianist. He portrayed us as trying to murder classical music. Maestro was furious. He wanted a public apology, wanted a confrontation, but his associates calmed him down. But this critic's point of view would be echoed by those of others. Lang Lang plays too much Lang Lang and not enough Beethoven. Lang Lang's Mozart sounds more Lang Lang than Mozart. Why must Lang Lang "Lang Lang–ize" everything he plays? Too personal, they wrote. Too subjective. Too schmaltzy. Too romantic. Too self-indulgent. Too undisciplined. I was being written about as a technical wizard but a self-absorbed interpreter.

Mr. Graffman told me not to read the words but to count the lines. The longer they write about you, he said, the better attention you get.

At least I'm being written about, I thought.

But Dad saw it differently. He cut out the articles and made me translate every one. He was especially interested in points made in the negative reviews.

"You must listen to these writers," he said. "They are learned men."

"They are idiots," I said.

"Even fools can teach us," said Dad.

My father and I argued long and hard about whether paying attention to the critics would help me or depress me.

I held my head high and kept playing. The offers kept coming, and I saw that, ironically, the criticism was helping. It made me controversial, and, funnily enough, controversy sells.

WITH DANIEL BARENBOIM AT
WALDBUHNE (BERLIN)

Maestro Barenboim

I believe the adage that says, "When the student is ready, the teacher appears." That certainly was true of my beloved professor Zhu, and the same was true of Professor Zhao. Without Gary Graffman, I would not have a career; he was my patient, loving, and deeply informed guide and guru who helped me navigate the transition from East to West. I have never encountered a pianist with a greater gift for shaping a phrase. And when I met Christoph Eschenbach in Ravinia, he too became a mentor and teacher, urging me to express my musical personality in everything I played. He gave me confidence, and his support was unwavering. When the critics attacked me for personalizing the pieces I played beyond the intention of the composers, Maestro said, "Follow your own path, be your own man." His piano technique was also a revelation: he is a liberal and spir-

WITH ZUBIN MEHTA AT THE
SCHLOSS SCHÖNBRUNN (VIENNA)

itual player whose pianissimos have the timbre of bells from heaven. He became, and remains, one of my constant collaborators. With Maestro conducting the Orchestre de Paris, I recorded Beethoven's Piano Concertos nos. 1 and 4, for which I later received my first Grammy nomination.

In September 2002, in New York, I met my next important mentor, after a performance with Maestro Loren Maazel, who had just begun his first season as music director of the New York Philharmonic. I had played Rachmaninoff's Piano Concerto no. 2 and was completely exhausted and about to leave my dressing room for the hotel when I heard a knock on the door. It was Zarin Mehta, director of the Ravinia Festival.

"I have someone I want you to meet." Zarin stepped aside and there stood Maestro Daniel Barenboim.

I had no idea he had been in the audience. Without thinking, I blurted out the words "Oh, Maestro, will you teach me?"

"Why, of course," he replied. I had never met the man before, and yet, as inappropriate as it may have seemed, I couldn't help but hug him. Right then and there I knew he'd change my musical outlook.

I related to Maestro Barenboim on many levels. First of all, he had been a child star, the most celebrated of his generation, who was playing piano recitals before his feet could reach the pedals. Born in Argentina, he became an Israeli citizen and, as far as I was concerned, a true citizen of the world. His piano skills were unparalleled, his repertoire leaned heavily on the German school, and as a conductor he had a repertoire that was nothing short of astounding—he had intimate knowledge of virtually every important composition in the classical canon.

Barenboim is also famous for using music to reconcile political tension. Although he was born a Jew during World War II and raised in Israel, he is known for his work with two great orchestras, the Chicago Symphony Orchestra and the Staatskapelle Berlin. He is also celebrated for his collaboration, in the name of peace and understanding, with the late Columbia University professor Edward Said, a Palestinian-American. From afar, I viewed Daniel Barenboim as a great man.

Close-up, he was down-to-earth and completely approachable. "Please call me Daniel," he said, "and feel free to get in touch with me whenever you like."

I took him at his word, and his word was golden. He became a true friend and tireless supporter. He also became a devoted teacher. Daniel taught me that emotions are indispensable ingredients in performing music but that overwrought emotionality can be injurious. The first job of the interpreter is to understand the structure of a piece. Structure is all. Daniel's sense of structure had come, in part, from his own teacher, Arthur Rubinstein. Amazing: One of my teachers—Gary Graffman—had been taught by Horowitz, and my new mentor was a student of Rubinstein's! I thanked the gods of good fortune.

Daniel taught me the German approach to the piano. In addition, he helped me understand Rubinstein. Rubinstein's sound, especially his playing of Chopin, was known for its sensitivity and warmth; it sounded like a human voice. In general the Russian style employs more arm movement, whereas the German style prefers solid fingers and far more intensity on the part of the hands.

Daniel had played all of the Beethoven sonatas when he was only sixteen years old, and he explained that while Beethoven is obviously emotional, when you play him you must look before you leap; you must control your mind before you're swept up by your feelings; you must weigh the two—emotional instinct and intellectual insight—and find the perfect balance. In Daniel's playing, that balance is always there. Daniel always reminded me to ask myself the deepest and most mystical questions: What is behind the notes? What is the intention? What is the meaning? What is the overall structure, in terms of both the compositional technique and the human story?

I had fallen in love with the Russian school. I had fallen in love with the French; when I played Debussy and Ravel, the extreme lightness of touch made me think of a breeze of fresh air, of Impressionist paintings and French perfume. Now, with Daniel's help, I was falling in love with the Germans.

With this new love of the Western European canon, I went to Vienna for the first time, in December 2002, to see Daniel's concert and to have my first lesson with him to prepare for an upcoming recording with Deutsche Grammophon. There I learned my first German words: "Guten Abend," meaning "Good evening," and "Vielen Danke," "Many thanks." In Vienna, I felt myself breathing in Mozart—his music is in the very air.

The night air on this particular evening was frosty cold. Snow was gently falling as I walked down cobblestoned streets, making it easy to pretend I was living in the eighteenth century. I was thinking of my future but was happy to be lost in the past. The shops intrigued me—the jewelers, the chocolatiers, the ancient stores selling sheet music alongside miniatures of Wolfgang Amadeus. Vienna's quiet charm put me in the best of moods, and when I turned a corner and saw, directly across the street, the reason I had come to this elegant city, tears filled my eyes. There it was: Wiener Musikverein, the Golden Hall, the center of Viennese musical culture and the residence of the Vienna Philharmonic, the hall from which its famous New Year's concert is broadcast each year.

Inside that magnificently gilded venue, I watched Daniel conduct the Vienna Philharmonic playing a Brahms symphony. He took my breath away. Back in Chicago, I continued to prepare with him for the recording: Daniel conducted the Chicago Symphony Orchestra, and I played, in memory of that night in Ravinia four short years ago, the Tchaikovsky Piano Concerto no. 1 and the Mendelssohn no. 1. To see my name on the album cover alongside Maestro Barenboim and the Chicago Symphony was humbling, but I must confess that humility turned to giddiness when, soon after its release, the record shot to the top of the Billboard classical chart. It was my first smash hit.

After this bestseller, my progress accelerated. Maestro Barenboim's careful instruction in the great works of the Western European canon was key in the expansion of my repertoire. Just as the Russians had so graciously accepted my interpretation of Rachmaninoff, the Germans were enamored of my Beethoven. Germany, along with China—my second concert there with the New York Philharmonic playing Rachmaninoff under Maestro Maazel totally blew them away—and the United States, became a primary venue for my performances. And yet I couldn't seem to enjoy my success.

Depression had been looming over me since my professional career took off. I'd felt constantly unmoored, always completely alone in spite of the crowds that clamored for my attention. I began feeling shaky and afraid. I worried about injuries. My biggest fear concerned my arms and hands. I worried I'd hurt myself badly and would no longer be able to play. If I couldn't play, I feared I'd go mad, there'd be no reason to live. Playing was the only thing that brought me joy. Every time I felt a twinge in my fingers or a tension in my arm, I was convinced that was it: the career-ending injury, the debilitating damage to my body that would render me useless for life.

And then it happened.

In 2003, a friend in New York had lent me a piano once used by Horowitz. To touch the very keys that had been touched by the master was, of course, a tremendous thrill, but because the ivory was worn and thin, I had to press the keys harder than I was used to. While practicing one evening, I struck the unyielding ivory especially forcefully, and a bolt of pain shot through my right pinkie and continued up my arm.

This was not my imagination. This was what I had long feared.

My father rushed me to a doctor, who told me I had played too many concerts and had practiced too much; I needed to rest my hand for a month. It was as if I'd been told not to eat for a month, but the doctor said that if I tried to play, I would be risking an even more severe injury.

A month without playing, with nothing to do but fixate on my injury. A month to worry. A month of fear.

Concerts had to be canceled. After one such cancellation, I got a surprise phone call from André Watts in Montreal. He had just been asked to substitute for me and was calling to make sure I was all right. He said, "You're doing pretty well—I'm now replacing you! I haven't played here for years, so thank you!" I couldn't help but think of the irony that the man for whom I had substituted was now substituting for me. But what would substitute for the piano that I could no longer play?

The first day was rough. I looked at the wall. I looked at my piano. Every fiber of my being was crying for me to play—but I stopped myself. I couldn't risk it. I thought of drug addicts who couldn't get a fix. I remembered someone calling that condition withdrawal. I had to remain active and engaged with the world around me or I'd go mad. I called the only person who'd ever succeeded in getting me to forget the piano, if only momentarily.

"This is great, Lang Lang," Dick Doran said when I explained my situation.

"How can you say that?"

"I say that because it's an opportunity."

"I'm afraid it's an opportunity for me to go nuts."

Dick laughed. "You won't go nuts. You'll learn what it's like to live a normal life. Your hand was injured because you don't live a balanced life."

Dick saw this as a chance for me to find balance, the kind that is at the heart of Chinese philosophy. The Chinese are masters at balancing, and so I turned to works by Confucius and Lao-tzu, and studied their different interpretations of yin and yang, which represent the two sides of human nature: female and male, dark and light, minor and major, introverted and extroverted, phoenix and dragon, rest and work. I filled my days watching TV, going to the movies, spending time with friends, and reading. Dick suggested that I read Shakespeare's history plays; he told me that Verdi had written an entire opera about Falstaff, and he thought I would be intrigued by Richard III, King John, and all the Henrys. He also brought me a book analyzing the big battles of World War II, which he knew was a passion of mine. He assured me that I would look back on this time as one of the greatest months of my life—a time to learn that I could live life without the piano.

I began with the book on World War II. Since my birth in 1982, there had been many wars in many parts of the world, but nothing like a world war. I was intrigued by the fact that only four decades before my birth the entire planet was aflame in conflict. The enormity of the struggle both horrified and fascinated me. Germany conquering France, Russia allied with America, the Japanese bombing Hawaii, the fighting in Asia and Africa—the sheer scope of the war had me reading and wondering for days.

Next I returned to Shakespeare. At first I resisted it; the language was difficult, and it wasn't a distraction from the pain and twinges in my fingers. But I pressed on and soon found myself caught up in the twisted personality of Richard III. I followed his bloody adventures, and when he was on the battlefield screaming, "A horse! A horse! My kingdom for a horse!" I was there with him, witnessing the end of the Wars of the Roses.

Friends visited. I took long walks around downtown Philadelphia. I went to the museums and stood in front of paintings. I studied a Picasso and found the music in the colors, then went home and listened to Gershwin and found the colors in the music. With friends I watched basketball and James Bond movies. I watched *8 Mile* with Eminem and finally understood the heated competition that drives hip-hop artists.

We saw Britney Spears at the Spectrum. The special effects were brilliant, the dancers gorgeous, and Britney super-sexy. I had a great time.

I caught up with what was happening in my friends' lives. Some were engrossed in their studies, others were not. We talked about what was wrong and what was right about our schools, our parents, our teachers. We gossiped. We went out for Chinese food. I even had time for girls. I had crushes on several girls and began to go on dates. One of the girls proved less intriguing than I had imagined; another was even more interesting than I had assumed. I had approached being a "normal" kid the way I approached practicing the piano; I thought I would need discipline, a plan, a schedule. Friends teased me and didn't believe I'd make the adjustment. But fairly quickly I began to enjoy myself, to panic less about the hours of practice I was missing, to immerse myself in the moment of whatever I was doing.

After a month, my hand had completely recovered. But all in all, the experience taught me a lot about myself. I discovered that I liked hanging out with friends, spending time alone reading, exploring the city, and watching movies and TV. I didn't have to practice ten hours a day to stay sane. And above all I learned that I could live with the fact that some critics might deplore my playing. It didn't feel good to acknowledge that fact, but it didn't kill me either. Was I ever really a normal teenager? Maybe not, but I also wasn't crazy. The piano is a beautiful thing, but during that month I learned that it isn't the only beautiful thing. Friends are beautiful. Shakespeare is beautiful. A slam dunk is beautiful. Dick Doran introduced me to the songs of Frank Sinatra, and they were beautiful too. More than a year after I graduated from Curtis, I had learned perhaps the most important lesson of my education: that balance is what matters most. It's a lesson I have tried to remain conscious of, even as the structure and demands of my life as a pianist threaten that balance every day. The world was now a totally different place, and much more interesting than it had been just a month earlier.

MY DAD AND ME
AT CARNEGIE HALL

Two Horses

The hall was empty, the stage bare except for a Steinway grand. In two hours, I would be seated at the piano and every seat in the house would be filled. The concert, my debut recital at Carnegie Hall in November 2003, had been sold out for months.

The solo appearance had arrived at a strange time in my career. At age twenty-one, I had begun to develop a fan base. The press had written about me a great deal, but increasingly critically. Some of the writers who had built me up were now tearing me down; they argued that I played melodramatically and that my interpretations were idiosyncratically personal and wrongheaded.

"Such criticism is to be expected," Mr. Graffman told me when he invited me to lunch at his apartment. "What else do they have to do? Criticism is their raison d'être."

I looked out the window across the street at Carnegie Hall; it was a fortress that had to be stormed and conquered. "I want to play so well," I told Mr. Graffman, "that even the most negative critic will have to admit my worth."

"Impossible," said Mr. Graffman. "Playing to please a critic is like thinking you can charm the devil. You can't out-think him and you can't out-charm him. All you can do is lose yourself in the greatness of the pieces you're playing."

Those pieces were indeed great: Schumann's Abegg Variations. Haydn's Piano Sonata in C Major, Schubert's "Wanderer" Fantasy. Chopin's Nocturne in D-flat Major, Liszt's *Réminiscences de Don Juan*, and Tan Dun's "Eight Memories in Watercolor, op. 1." I had chosen them for both variety and beauty. To sit onstage with a full symphony behind you, filling every space in the auditorium with sound, is one thing. To provide that sound entirely by yourself is quite another. Of course I was well accustomed to recitals at this point in my career, but Carnegie Hall was a singular experience. It had to be perfect.

I believe it was. The audience seemed to believe it was. The ovations were long, warm, and sincere. I could not have been more pleased. When it came time for encores, though, I had already decided that along with playing Liszt's "Liebestraum" and Schumann's "Träumerei," I wanted to do something special. I wanted to play a duet with my father. When he was young, my father's dream, like that of most musicians, had been to play at Carnegie Hall; yet his musical ambitions had been thwarted. For my entire life, my father had always been there, every step of the way, helping me to achieve my dream; despite the truly terrible times we had been through, the times I'd hated and resented him, I would not have had a career in music were it not for him—the career that became my own dream. By playing with him at Carnegie Hall, I could give him back something in gratitude. And besides, he is a fine musician, and I knew the audience would appreciate him; we would have fun together.

To New York ears, the erhu is an exotic instrument, and Dad plays it brilliantly. We chose a Chinese composition called "Competing Horses" or "Horse Race," and for the program I changed the name to "Two Horses," because we'd arranged it for two instruments. The vibrant piece, in which the piano and the erhu create the sound of racing stallions, allowed my father to demonstrate his virtuosity, and he did so in grand style. Holding hands and bowing with him as we received a standing ovation, I couldn't help but think how far we had come together—it was a moment of great triumph and reconciliation.

While the pain of our past had not left me, the very nature of my relationship with my father had changed. In the six years since we had arrived in Philadelphia, the shift had been dramatic. In China, my dad was my boss. In America, I had slowly but surely become his boss. To Dad's credit, he accepted this role gracefully. He understood, largely because all my business dealings outside China were conducted in English, that I was more competent than he to handle my affairs. More important, he recognized my ability to do so and stood behind me every step of the way. I was the one meeting with my managers, my record label, and my publicists. I was directing my own career, making my own decisions, and hoping that my father would acquiesce to a subservient role. When he did, my respect for him grew. His devotion had been tested once again, and once again he passed the test, even at the expense of his considerable ego.

Beyond Music

$\mathcal{S}$ince I've established my professional career, my life has been a whirlwind of constant travel, excitement, and even glamour. The reality of it goes beyond even what I dreamed of as a child. I live in airplanes, streaking back and forth from Berlin to Beijing, Buenos Aires to Seoul, New York to Tokyo, from the Golden Globe Awards ceremony to the World Cup to a concert at the Nobel Prize ceremony to the Grammys. I have played at the Kremlin and the White House, before the queen of England and six times before President Hu Jintao of China. I debuted with the Berlin Philharmonic, led by Sir Simon Rattle at the Waldbuhne, before an audience of twenty thousand; I performed with the Vienna Phil-

harmonic under Maestro Zubin Mehta at the Schönbrunn Palace, the summer palace of the Austro-Hungarian Empire, before an audience of a hundred thousand. I am met at airports and

UNICEF GOODWILL
AMBASSADOR LANG LANG

whisked to luxurious suites in opulent hotels. I have drivers wherever I go and people eager to accommodate me in any way possible. I eat at the best restaurants. I am invited to play in the finest concert halls accompanied by the finest musicians. It's crazy, nonstop, and I love it.

I rejoice at my good fortune and blessed life. I love bringing my music to hundreds of thousands of people, to help inspire their love of classical music. I am honored to be a member of a generation of Chinese musicians born in the 1980s whose mission is to play classical music beautifully, with heart, soul, and enlightened mind.

And yet . . .

My life is confined to airplanes, hotels, and concert halls. Because classical music has always been the product of cities and its audience has always been primarily the educated and well-to-do, my life is lived out in the most affluent and advanced urban centers in the world. I go to London, Hamburg, Chicago, Vienna, Tel Aviv, and St. Petersburg because that's where I'm invited, where the symphony orchestras play, and where the music lovers live. If I have a few hours to spare, I'll tour the cities. But because I am learning new pieces on the road while relearning old ones, my time is limited. I see Dallas or Stockholm from the back of a car, I get fleeting glimpses of billboards and pedestrians, and I can't help but wonder about the rest of the world. What's happening in the villages and the countryside? When I was a child, it was hard to see a world beyond music, precisely because music *was* my world. But now that I'm out in the world, I have to wonder what's out there beyond the luxury hotels and restaurants. I can never forget where I've come from—the poverty, the loneliness. Those early years in Beijing shaped me. When music critics claimed that I was too ambitious and eager to learn, I consoled myself with the thought that were it not for his desire to eat well, Mozart—to name just one composer—would not have written as much as he had. And I do what I can. Whenever I am in a city for more than a day or two, I make sure to give master classes or children's concerts, to try to introduce and inspire a new generation of classical music lovers. One of my ideas to make music more fun for kids was to create, with Steinway, versions of a "Lang Lang Steinway"—upright and baby grand pianos with chalk boards on which they can write a poem or their feelings, or draw pictures inspired by the music they play. They have become very popular in China. But I want to do more.

In 2004, my dear friend Nora Benary, who worked at the United Nations, seeing my enthusiasm with children, introduced me to the executive director of the United Nations Children's Fund, who invited me to become an International Goodwill Ambassador to UNICEF. A few months later I was greatly honored to be appointed as the youngest ambassador to UNICEF in its history. In my role, I would travel to different parts of the world and see the devastating effects AIDS and other diseases have on children. I immediately told my management office that for two weeks in August, I would not be available for concerts. I went to the doctor to get malaria shots and the next day flew to Tanzania.

The trip began with difficulty. The malaria shot gave me a high fever, and that first night was rough. The next morning, after a fitful sleep, I opened my eyes and saw nothing but water—sparkling blue water as far as I could see. I was looking at the Indian Ocean. A faint mist hung in the air, and through my feverish eyes the world appeared dreamlike, unspoiled, and precious. We had arrived in Dar es Salaam, a town whose Arabic name means Peaceful City.

A local doctor gave me some natural remedy, and my fever broke quickly. Within twenty-four hours, we took a helicopter to Zanzibar, the archipelago just off the coast of East Africa that is part of Tanzania, and from there flew in a helicopter to Kilimanjaro. There I got into a jeep with a UNICEF flag waving from the radio antenna and drove three hours to a village suffering from abject poverty. We were introduced to various tribes, but the Masai, a tall and elegant people with exquisitely long, expressive faces, especially intrigued me. I was the first

Chinese person many of them had ever seen, and they closely examined the shape of my eyes and the color of my skin. When we reached the children's school, I saw signs that said, "Welcome Home, UNICEF Ambassador Lang Lang." Inside the schoolhouse, the kids gathered around me, and when they were told that I played an instrument, they brought out their own—stringed and percussive—and started to play. I loved their rhythms. The children put on a play about the dangers of AIDS and all that they had been taught about the terrible disease. I could see that some of those in the play were already suffering from its effects. When I had to leave, they ran after my jeep, shouting warm farewells.

I had so many unforgettable experiences. A sky safari allowed me to see hundreds of zebras, lions, tigers, leopards, and flamingos as we surveyed the land from a low-flying helicopter. Health ministers and physicians in various villages educated me about the ways in which AIDS was devastating the population, especially the children—the same children who cooked for us and danced for us and, through an interpreter, told us stories, some happy, some tragic. I could feel their need to be seen and heard. In another village we watched another play put on by children: a boy forces a girl to have sex, and the girl becomes pregnant and is expelled from school, kicked out of her home, and shunned by her friends. It was a heartbreaking drama that became the focal point of a dialogue between me and the kids. We discussed the immorality of rape, the hypocrisy of social institutions, the intolerance of family and friends. The children were curious, intelligent, and introspective. Mostly, they were grateful for the presence of an openhearted listener.

I met many Europeans who had come to Tanzania to teach. Back in Zanzibar, which is largely Muslim, there's something of a musical colloquy. Teachers from Egypt, India, Germany, and the United States introduced me to the history of the islands through their songs. Their students play, sing, and dance a mix of beguiling styles from the world over. I'd call them charming, but the emotional impact on me was far deeper than that. Within the souls of these African students I saw a reservoir of shining spirit and abundant talent.

I spent the evening in a home that had the architectural characteristics of a mosque. The ceilings were high and the mosaics intricate. I climbed to the top of one of the minarets and stepped out onto the tiny balcony. There, facing the vast Indian Ocean, I watched the sun melt into the sea, the sky turning from orange to pink to misty blue, and I heard the chanting of prayers from inside the mosque. I found myself crying. I felt confused that the human condition could be so wondrous yet so appalling.

On my last day, I went back to Dar es Salaam, where we held a news conference so I could report on what I had learned. I tried to be clear and succinct, and to hold back my tears. At the end, someone rolled out a piano and I was asked to play. I started with simple Chinese songs. The kids went wild, jumping up and down and touching the piano as though it were magical. They were giddy, the way I had been when I first saw *Tom and Jerry* as a boy in Shenyang.

During that trip, I often thought of my own difficult childhood, but my days and nights in Africa redefined the meaning of difficulty and put many things in perspective for me. I kept remembering what Kofi Annan, the UN secretary-general, had told me in New York before I'd left for Africa. "Lang Lang," he said, "your responsibility as an artist goes beyond music. Your art must serve people and peace."

They are words I try to live by, whether when performing or simply interacting with other people. I try to stay involved in issues regarding my beloved China, a country experiencing one of the most dramatic economic growths in recorded history, where with that growth have arisen ecological and environmental issues of staggering proportions: water shortage, waste, soil erosion, desertification, air pollution. Recently, I became an environmental ambassador for China. I lent my support to organizations within China to raise public awareness and became a spokesman for a cause advocating the urgent need for alternative energies. As the world changes, we need to be responsive and engaged.

The world of music is also changing daily, and we will have to figure out how to keep classical music alive and thriving in this multimedia, digital new age. I'm eager to see how the future of classical music evolves, and I'd like to have a role in its future. I am currently developing a foundation to support the inspirational education of classical music—but my foundation will go beyond music. I'm interested in working with artists of different disciplines and of different musical backgrounds to see how we can all work together to help children realize their dreams, with music as a starting point. Music is the true connector; the world of music is truly a world without borders. My journey in Africa taught me that lesson: before it, I thought mostly of my own career; now I see my role as a musician as that of a cultural ambassador who can build bridges between cultures and foster peaceful and respectful cooperation. After all, musicians need to play together.

I have always dreamed big. And while it may seem idealistic or naive to believe that I can improve the world by improving the lives of children through music, I remind myself of the saying of Lao-tzu: that a journey of a thousand miles begins with a single step. By now, I have journeyed far more than a thousand miles as I travel from city to city sharing music. And yet my journey is still only beginning.

Acknowledgments

Thank you to David Ritz, Jean Jacques Cesbron, Steve Rubin, Cindy Spiegel, and the entire Spiegel & Grau team. I would also like to thank my family members, friends, mentors, teachers, fellow artists, and all of the people who have supported me.

Printed in the United States
by Baker & Taylor Publisher Services